# Managing Public Involvement in Healthcare Purchasing

## Health Services Management

*Series Editors:*
*Chris Ham,* Health Services Management Centre, University of Birmingham
*Chris Heginbotham,* East and North Hertfordshire Health Agency

The British National Health Service is one of the biggest and most complex organizations in the developed world. Employing around one million people and accounting for £36 billion of public expenditure, the service is of major concern to both the public and politicians. Management within the NHS faces a series of challenges in ensuring that resources are deployed efficiently and effectively. The challenges include the planning and management of human resources, the integration of professionals into the management process, and making sure that services meet the needs of patients and the public.

Against this background, the Health Services Management series addresses the many issues and practical problems faced by people in managerial roles in health services.

*Current and forthcoming titles*

# Managing Public Involvement in Healthcare Purchasing

*Carol Lupton, Stephen Peckham and Pat Taylor*

**Open University Press**
*Buckingham • Philadelphia*

Open University Press
Celtic Court
22 Ballmoor
Buckingham
MK18 1XW

email: enquiries@openup.co.uk
world wide web: http://www.openup.co.uk

and

325 Chestnut Street
Philadelphia, PA 19106, USA

First Published 1998

A catalogue record of this book is available from the British Library

ISBN   0 335 19633 0 (hb)   0 335 19632 2 (pb)

*Library of Congress Cataloging-in-Publication Data*
Lupton, Carol.
    Managing public involvement in healthcare purchasing / Carol
Lupton, Stephen Peckham, and Pat Taylor.
        p.    cm. — (Health services management)
    Includes bibliographical references and index.
    ISBN 0–335–19633–0 (hardcover). — ISBN 0–335–19632–2 (pbk.)
    1. Fundholding (Medical economics)—Great Britain—Citizen
participation.   2. Medical policy—Great Britain—Citizen
participation.   I. Peckham, Stephen.   II. Taylor, Pat. 1948 May 15–
III. Title.   IV. Series.
RA410.55.G7L87   1998
362.1'0941—dc21                                                   97–44933
                                                                           CIP

Typeset by Graphicraft Typesetters Ltd, Hong Kong
Printed in Great Britain by St Edmundsbury Press Ltd,
Bury St Edmunds, Suffolk

# Contents

# Acknowledgements

Acknowledgement must be made of the NHS Executive (South and West) Responsive mode R & D committee which provided the funding for much of the empirical work on which this text is based, and to all those respondents across the former Wessex region who gave so willingly of their time. Grateful thanks to my colleagues Rob Atkinson, Norman Johnson and Andrew Massey for their helpful comments on my chapter drafts, and to Mark for his overall support and advice. Thanks finally to Pauline and David, without whose practical help this book would never have seen the light of day.

*Carol Lupton*

My acknowledgements to Anne for putting up with all my evenings at the computer and to my co-authors for their effort and ideas. I would also like to acknowledge all the people in the health service and community and voluntary groups I have worked with over the years who have helped my understanding of the issues.

*Stephen Peckham*

I would like to thank Andy Friedman for his help and support in reading and commenting on drafts of my chapters and my administrative colleagues at the University of the West of England for their technical support and unfailing patience under pressure. Finally I would like to thank my co-authors for their extreme forbearance in working with me.

*Pat Taylor*

# Preface

The National Health Service presents a paradox. Of all the public services it can have the greatest personal impact on members of the public . . . But no public service thinks less about the public as such: to the NHS the public are patients.

(Nairne 1984: 33)

This book is about the nature of the 'paradox of the public' within the National Health Service (NHS). In the years since Nairne – one time Permanent Secretary at the former Department of Health and Social Security – wrote these words, the NHS has undergone significant organizational and cultural changes. Although still publicly funded, the service has been remodelled more closely on private sector lines, with separate purchaser and provider organizations operating in market-like conditions. In this new healthcare marketplace, the patient is recast as health 'consumer' with new rights – to choice, redress and information – characteristic of his/her commercial counterpart. Via mechanisms such as *The Patient's Charter* (DoH 1991), these new rights are explicitly designed to shift the balance of power between patients and professionals and between service users and providers/purchasers. The decentralization of decision making, the rise of primary care-based purchasing and the formal role of healthcare purchasers as 'champion of the people', may all be seen to have enhanced the potential responsiveness of the service to local needs and afforded the public a more visible and influential role in its overall development.

The changing shape of the NHS, however, may have served to reformulate rather than resolve the paradox identified by Nairne. The more active role of the consumer may have replaced that of the passive patient, but the essentially individualistic nature of the role remains largely unchanged. The increased commitment to identifying the wishes of individual consumers has not generally been matched by a determination to enhance the responsiveness of the service to the collective views of local communities and the wider public. The ascendancy of the new consumerism indeed has been accompanied by the waning role of more traditional forms of public involvement in the service as local authority membership on health authority boards is ended, the work of the community health councils is politically constrained and the activities of user and health interest groups are viewed with organizational suspicion. As this book will demonstrate, as the NHS moves towards the end of the twentieth century, it is increasingly bedevilled by growing public concern about the opaqueness of its decision-making processes, the probity of its stewardship and the extent of its accountability to the public. Subject to greater central control and scrutiny, purchasers are struggling to develop the role of people's champion in the face of a growing 'democratic deficit' at the local level.

This book sets out to improve our understanding of the issues surrounding public involvement in healthcare purchasing and to inform and encourage more effective strategies for its future development. In doing so, the text inevitably raises wider issues about the nature of public sector services and the appropriate roles of the state, the market, professionals and the public in its many guises (citizens, consumers and communities). In the face of the challenge by the New Right to the ideals of collectivism, it ultimately raises more fundamental questions about the kind of society we want to live in and the responsibilities we have to each other and to the social community as a whole. In particular, it causes us to assess whether services such as health and social care are to be seen as collective goods, funded by us all on the basis of our common interest, or essentially private commodities, provided via the market in response to our personal choices as self-interested individuals. The reality, of course, lies somewhere in between these two extremes; the precise point at which the balance is struck in the specific case of health is a recurrent theme of the chapters that follow.

The first three chapters of the book address the broader issues and wider context of public involvement in health in terms of three key dimensions: agency, structure and process. In Chapter 1, we explore the debates surrounding the relationship between the state and the individual and the very different rights and responsibilities contained in the contrasting roles of citizen and consumer. We assess the strengths and weaknesses of both market and popular democratic approaches to public involvement and consider the argument that new ways need to be found to revitalize the role of 'the people' in public sector services. Chapter 2 examines the profound changes characterizing the development of the public sector in the UK over the years of the 1980s and 1990s. We describe how the organizational shape of the NHS has been moulded by the wider political objective of shifting the boundaries between state and market and between public and private responsibility. In Chapter 3, we consider the implications of the internal market and new public management approaches for the enduring tensions within the NHS between central and local lines of accountability and between professional, political and managerial power and control.

The different types and levels of public involvement and the different expectations and assumptions by which they are underpinned are examined in Chapter 4. The contrast between democratic and consumerist approaches, in terms of their use of concepts such as power, empowerment, representation and accountability, is highlighted. We then trace the key themes and issues characterizing the development of lay involvement in public services over the post-war years. In Chapter 5, we look at the history of public involvement in the specific context of the NHS, reflecting how little institutional interest there was in the role of the public over the first twenty years of the service's development. We then chart the growth of patient and health interest groups and community and new public health movements in the years of the 1980s and into the 1990s and consider how this has coincided with the new managerialist interest in the public as consumer within the NHS marketplace. In Chapter 6, we focus specifically on the continually changing context of healthcare purchasing within the NHS. We describe the recent move to primary care or GP-led commissioning and question the implication for public involvement of the greater fragmentation of purchasing which may result.

Chapters 7 and 8 are based on the findings of a number of different empirical studies undertaken by the authors of the contemporary role of the public in healthcare purchasing. Chapter 7 examines the way in which, and extent to which, health purchasers have set about discharging their role as proxy consumers in the healthcare marketplace and describes the particular techniques and approaches they have employed to do so. Our central concern here is to assess the extent and implications of the current balance which obtains between central political requirements emphasizing predominantly individual and 'consumerist' approaches to public involvement, on the one hand, and pressures for more participatory and collective initiatives, on the other, as purchasers seek local support and legitimization. Chapter 8 considers the response of the public, in its many forms, to the involvement initiatives developed by healthcare purchasers for the 1990s. The chapter describes the kinds of individuals who get involved, their motivations for doing so and the dilemmas and difficulties they experience as a result. Throughout the chapter, emphasis is given to those aspects of the organizational approach that appear to inhibit and those that appear to encourage, the effective participation of the public.

Chapter 9 provides the conclusion to the book by summarizing the key issues for purchasers attempting to develop public involvement in the face of the different, and potentially contradictory, imperatives of the wider consumerist/democratic and policy/operational frameworks. The implications of the new forms of purchasing emerging in the late 1990s are assessed and attention is given to the question of whether the different layers of operational, locality and strategic purchasing may similarly require different types of public involvement strategies. The chapter concludes by returning to the central question posed in this introduction: why should the public be involved in the NHS? The answer we provide is twofold: because public involvement is essential for the organizational health of the service and because, as a process, it is a means by which the wider political and social health of the nation may be enhanced.

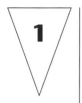

# 1 Health and citizenship

## Introduction

> Everyone has the right to a standard of living adequate for the health
> and well being of himself and his family, including food, clothing, hous-
> ing and medical care . . .
> (Universal Declaration of Human Rights, Article 25)

As the above Declaration makes clear, access to healthcare must be considered a basic human right, a necessary prerequisite of an individual's
ability fully to participate in social life and a central attribute of social
and political citizenship. The years of the twentieth century saw a growing international acknowledgement of the responsibility of the state to
ensure the health of its citizens. Across most Western democracies, national
health systems were established as part of the more general 'welfare settlement' which followed the Second World War. While individual nation
states differed in terms of the nature and extent of state involvement, most
accepted the need at least to ensure a minimum of collective provision for
those not otherwise able to provide for themselves. As T.H. Marshall
(1965: 115) argued in the mid-1960s: 'No modern government can dis-
claim a general responsibility for the health of its people, nor would it
wish to do so'.

The definition of 'health', however, ranges widely, from the fairly minimal
– the absence of ill health and the prevention of disease – to the more
comprehensive definition provided in the constitution of the World Health
Organization as 'a state of complete physical, mental and social well-being
and not merely the absence of disease' (WHO 1985: 87). Over the post-
war years, the demand for healthcare, and for maximum rather than minimum forms of provision, grew steadily, stimulated by demographic change,

by scientific and technological progress and by the rising expectations of increasingly affluent populations. In the face of continued global economic recession, however, the ability of individual nation states to respond to this demand was increasingly constrained. Rising political anxiety about the cost of health expenditure, combined with reduced public tolerance of poor quality provision, prompted the search for new and better methods of organizing and delivering services. In particular, the post-war dominance of collectivist assumptions about the role of the state in healthcare was increasingly challenged by pluralist and individualist approaches emphasizing the need for diversity rather than uniformity and for individual rather than state reliance. A key force behind this challenge was the growing international influence of the ideas of the political Right.

This chapter describes the key principles and inherent tensions underpinning the development of the UK National Health Service (NHS). The nature of the New Right challenge to 'collectivism' is examined and the 'market' and 'political' models of health policy are compared. Assessment is then made of the implications of the different approaches, and the contrasting roles of consumer and citizen contained within them, for the involvement of the public in healthcare systems.

## The rise of collectivism

> A free health service is a triumphant example of the superiority of collective action and public initiative applied to a segment of society where commercial principles are seen at their worst.
>
> (Bevan 1978: 109)

Bevan's contrast between 'collective action' and 'commercial principles' reflects two very different ideal-typical models of healthcare policy: the 'collectivist' (or political) and the 'market'. Collectivist healthcare systems are characterized by extensive state intervention, a commitment to universality of entitlement and equality of access and funded through general taxation rather than by individual insurance. In the market model, healthcare is predominantly insurance-based, with the administration of services largely in private hands and the role of the state limited to regulation or residual direct provision. These two policy models are underpinned by very different ideological assumptions about both the nature of health and the relationship between the individual and the state. In the market model, health is seen as essentially a private responsibility, and healthcare viewed as a commodity like any other whose distribution between individuals can be governed by the mechanisms of competition and exchange; in the collectivist model, health is conceptualized as a 'public good', a collective responsibility, whose equitable distribution is secured by the processes of popular democracy. This difference is encapsulated by Marshall (1965: 128) in his opposition to the idea of charges for healthcare: 'It would treat sickness as a personal liability and medical care as a special kind of consumer good, instead of treating sickness as a misfortune and medical care as a community service'.

These two models, of course, exist nowhere in their pure form. As a means of categorizing different healthcare systems, they should more accurately be seen as two ends of a continuum with countries such as the UK, Sweden and Italy being located closer to the 'collectivist' end of the spectrum and those of the United States and Australia being nearer to the market model. Whatever their location on this continuum, the healthcare systems of all Western democracies were characterized in the post-war years by an increased extent of state involvement. Even that flagship of free enterprise and individualistic voluntary insurance, the United States, found it necessary to provide a collective response to the needs of the elderly, those with a disability and those living below the poverty line – the 'medically needy' – via the 'Medicare' and 'Medicaid' provisions as well as to impose some government regulation of the private healthcare market. Wall (1996) identifies three main motivations for increased government involvement in healthcare systems: to provide a reasonable standard of care; to ensure equity of access; and to encourage the effective allocation of resources. In addition, she argues, the relatively high and unpredictable nature of the 'costs' of health treatment and care has necessitated some level of collective funding in all liberal democracies. Again, even in the United States, it is the case that 'a considerable proportion' of medical expenses is met by public funds (Chandler 1996: 170).

As we have indicated, the National Health Service developed in the UK after the Second World War was explicitly collectivist in nature. Thus the White Paper establishing the service in 1944 talked proudly of '...the creation of a new public responsibility; to make it in future somebody's clear duty to see that all medical facilities are available to all people' (Ministry of Health 1944: 47). Marshall (1965) summarizes the four clear principles underpinning the NHS: that basic services are free at the point of consumption; that the right to the service is universal; that all those who use the service get the same treatment; and that the service provided is the best that the economy can provide. The universal and comprehensive service so planned, with eligibility extending to everyone as a basic right of citizenship, involved the rejection of the individual, insurance-based approaches of the past in which certain groups were covered and others excluded. Funding from national taxes would ensure the pooling of risks between the sick and the healthy as well as provide for a progressive redistribution of costs between the poor and the rich. The aim was 'to divorce the care of health from questions of personal means or other factors irrelevant to it' (Marshall 1965: 127). Equality of access to care, moreover, carried with it an important commitment to 'territorial justice', in which the existing spatial inequalities of health provision would be removed by central planning and administration. The service would also be comprehensive in the sense that it would cover all aspects of a particular course of treatment and the full range of available services.

Many commentators, however, have noted the only limited extent to which this collectivist vision was implemented. The principle of a free service was eroded from the start by the introduction of a prescription charge in 1949, for example, and little explicit reference was made in the legislation to the idea of equity, over and above that of equality of entitlement. As Powell (1996) comments, in reality the operation of NHS was more about vertical equity between the sick and the well, the young and the old, than about the horizontal redistribution of income between the rich and the poor. Financial constraints over the early development of the service, moreover, served to reinforce rather than remove the spatial inequalities of health and only with the Hospital Plan of 1962 was there any coherent attempt to achieve some national measure of distribution according to need. Most importantly, while the service may have been comprehensive in terms of its coverage, it was not so in terms of the services made available. Ultimately, treatment for some types of conditions and certain kinds of patients could be withheld on the basis of clinical judgements. The rights represented in the establishment of the NHS were not thus to healthcare itself, but only to the access to professional assessment.

This brings us to one of the central dilemmas at the heart of the collectivist approach: the means by which the public or collective interest is to be represented. In what he calls the 'paternalist' approach, Klein (1980) argues the language of 'wants' characteristic of the market model is transformed into the language of 'needs'. In the context of the NHS, the identification of those needs and the nature of society's response to them is placed in the hands of a powerful sectional interest group: the medical profession. While in theory the 'public good' may be ensured by the state as the representative of the people, in reality it is defined and operationalized by the 'expert': As Harrison and Pollitt (1994: 35) remind us: '. . . the shape of the total service provided by the NHS was the aggregate outcome of individual doctors' clinical decisions, rather than the result of decisions made by politicians, policy-makers, planners or managers.' This situation, Klein argues, introduces a central 'internal contradiction' within the NHS in which the reduction of the public interest to the sum of clinical judgements inevitably gave rise to pressures to remove or insulate the service from the political process:

> If there is an overriding collective interest, a public good which is different from the aggregation of individual private goods, and if that public good is further defined by experts, then it follows that the system should be insulated from everyday political pressures.
>
> (Klein 1980: 130)

The contradiction between political and professional power, moreover, was overlain in the establishment of the NHS by a further tension between the centralized administration of the service, in pursuit of improved efficiency and national equity, and its control at a local level in the name of democratic accountability and responsiveness. Unwilling to submit to democratic control, the medical profession lobbied heavily against placing the administration of the service in the hands of the local authorities. The compromise reached, which combined central political control with local authority representation on medically-dominated health authorities, involved an uneasy truce between two contrasting imperatives which, as Klein (1989: 28) has argued, was to represent an ongoing contradiction within the NHS: 'a continuing and never-ending attempt to reconcile what may well turn out to be irreconcilable aims of policy'. We shall return to these issues throughout this book.

The initial political enthusiasm for the welfare state in the UK began to crumble in the face of the adverse economic conditions following the Second World War. Concerns grew about the excessive cost of public expenditure and, as an editorial in the *British Medical Journal* made clear at the time, the 'extravagant' NHS was identified as a principal culprit: 'The NHS is heading for the bankruptcy court . . . and we are facing bankruptcy because of the Utopian finances of the Welfare State' (*BMJ* 1950: 148). As the social problems and financial costs of post-war reconstruction grew, the tide turned against the view that publicly provided health and welfare services would be an enduring feature of social life. The 1950s were thus a period of caution and slow growth in which expenditure on housing and education was given priority over that on health. Despite the report of a government Committee in 1953 recommending additional expenditure on the NHS (Guillebaud 1956), political concern about the cost of the service continued to grow. Increasingly it became clear that Bevan's assumption that the demand for services would level off as the population grew healthier was fundamentally misplaced. The NHS was thus seen to be caught in a 'financial treadmill' (Leathard 1990) as an apparently limitless demand was driven by demographic change (particularly the rise in the number of elderly people), technological and scientific advances and increased public expectations. Even so, a subsequent Royal Commission into the cost of the NHS reported in 1979 that the service continued to represent good value for money and, whilst noting the need for a more efficient use of resources, recommended further increases in expenditure. As Butler (1992) concludes, despite its growing cost, the predominately collectivist nature of the NHS remained largely unaltered over the years of the 1960s and 1970s:

> In its fundamentals and in many of its details, the NHS would still have been recognisable to the founding fathers of the welfare state as the egalitarian machine they had struggled hard to create.
>
> (Butler 1992: 55)

However, by the 1980s things were beginning to change. The slow and uneven recovery which took place after the global economic crisis of the 1970s caused a wave of 'fiscal conservatism' to wash across most western post-industrial nations. The collapse of Keynesian macro-economic management and the failure of centralized social planning combined finally to dismantle the post-war social democratic consensus on the need for state intervention to ensure social and economic prosperity. The 1980s saw a growing anxiety about the size and inefficiency of the state and the financial burden it was placing on national economies. This anxiety was heightened on the part of politicians by the emergence of more prosperous and tax-conscious electorates. The result was an international reassessment of the appropriate nature and extent of state activity that questioned the accepted balance between the public and the private spheres and between political and market processes. As we shall see, this reassessment was to have profound implications for the UK public sector in general and the NHS in particular.

## The challenge of the 'new liberalism'

> The Soviet Union is the immediate danger perceived by the Americans. Yet it is not the real threat to our national security. The real threat is the welfare state.
>
> (Friedman and Friedman 1985: 73)

A central influence on the redefinition of the role of the state in the provision of healthcare has been the growing international dominance of the ideas of the radical right or the 'new liberals'. Although characterized by a variety of different strands of thought, all are united in a criticism of what is viewed as the unquestioned growth of the modern service state and its involvement, some would say interference, in all aspects of social and economic life. For influential writers such as Milton Friedman and the Chicago School (see Green (1987) for an accessible exposition of this and other variants of the new liberalism) the primary cause of the distortion of the role of the state is the operation of the pluralist democratic process. This serves to 'ratchet up' the volume of state activity as politicians struggle to accommodate the various demands of growing numbers of competing interest groups. The resulting growth of government expenditure, particularly on health and welfare services, places increasing demands on the national income which become ever more difficult to meet. The growth of the modern state is thus viewed as both parasitical and destructive:

> The public sector, including central and local government, and more accurately named the state sector or wealth-eating sector . . . spread like bindweed at the expense of the non-state sector, the wealth-creating sector, strangling and threatening to destroy what it grew upon.
>
> (Keith Joseph, cited in Cutler and Waine 1994: 105)

From the new liberal perspective, the size and cost of state activity is further extended by the activities of two key sectional interest groups. The first is the cadre of public officials whose primary objective is not to serve the public but rather to maximize their own budgets and status. The second is the growing 'army of experts' – the privileged professional groups – working within the state, who it is argued exercise a state licensed 'restraint of trade' through the monopoly of provision. As with the so-called public servant these professionals are seen to serve their own group interests via restricted access, enhanced job security, rigid work practices and by deliberately encouraging dependency on the part of those who receive their services. The result, it is argued, is an 'iron triangle' of bureaucrats, poverty professionals and state beneficiaries whose mutually reinforcing interests dominate the policy process.

A major problem for the New Right is the obsession of the modern state with the promotion of equality. This objective is seen to be both inappropriate and inequitable. While the new liberals do not argue with the importance of formal equality before the law, nor even (for some) equality of opportunity, the problem as they see it is the pursuit of equality of outcome. This is not only impossible insofar as we can never ensure that everyone has an identical supply of public goods such as housing, health and education, but it is also essentially self-defeating insofar as the pursuit of equality of outcome actually serves to further the interests of the few who are in a position successfully to manipulate the political process. Any attempt to redistribute the national income, it is argued, is more likely to benefit the well placed and articulate middle classes than to ameliorate the plight of the poor: 'Public expenditures are made primarily for the benefit of the middle class, and financed with taxes which are borne in considerable part by the poor and the rich' (Friedman and Friedman 1980: 107).

Welfare services are further criticized by the ideologues of the New Right not just because of their cost, but also because they are seen adversely to affect the nature of the relationship between the state and the individual. The proliferation of state benefits and other welfare services, it is argued, serves to erode individual responsibility and self-reliance, with the 'perverse consequence' of maintaining rather than alleviating the poverty and inequality they were designed to combat. The provision of state benefits adds to the disorganization and demoralization of the poor – fostering their dependence and sapping their determination to improve their situation:

> ... dependence in the long run decreases human happiness and reduces human freedom ... the well-being of individuals is best protected and promoted when they are helped to be independent, to use their talents to take care of themselves and their families, and to achieve things on their own.
>
> (Moore 1987: 5)

Rather than creating dependency, the state must encourage greater individual self-reliance and the only way to do this is to end the monopoly of state provision. Monopolistic services inhibit choice and prevent the possibility of 'exit'; they must be replaced by arrangements that empower individuals to provide for themselves and their families. The right to security and equality must be replaced by the right to risk and responsibility and to be free from interference by the state. For the new liberals, only the unfettered operation of the market can guarantee these rights. Although it may mean that some individuals are able to achieve more than others, the neutral mechanism of the market prevents the institutionalization of inequalities of wealth by maximizing the ability of all individuals to secure and protect their own interests. Far from being the creator of poverty, capitalism is, in fact, the means by which the living standards of the poor can and have been steadily improved. Markets cannot cause social injustice; for something to be unjust it has to be the result of deliberate action and, because they are based on free exchange, the outcomes of market processes are unintended. It is interference with the market in the interests of particular sectional groups that produces injustice. By securing individual freedom, the market offers the poor a better chance to improve their situation: '[the market] . . . preserves the opportunity for today's disadvantaged to become tomorrow's privileged and, in the process, enables everyone, from top to bottom, to enjoy a fuller and richer life' (Friedman and Friedman 1980: 148–9).

## The New Right and healthcare

As we have seen, for the New Right there are few public goods that cannot be provided by the market, apart from those needed to protect basic civil freedoms such as defence and criminal justice. The provision of healthcare is no exception, despite the fact that it is typically claimed as the supreme example of the need for public rather than private provision. The New Right challenge the basic 'collectivist' assumption that healthcare services must be provided free because the market would introduce inequalities based on ability to pay. Their argument is that state provision is not the most effective way of protecting the interest of the poor because it serves to increase the cost and diminish the quality of the service provided to everyone, poor and rich alike. The removal of the mechanism of 'price' within health services means that the individual consumer is not restricted in his/her demand for services and this serves to ratchet up the use and thus the cost of healthcare, creating: 'an unreal world in which resources that are scarce and should be rationed have been made to appear plentiful because they are supplied "free"' (Seldon, in Green 1987: 178). Lack of competition further exacerbates the cost of the service as providers face no incentives to improve efficiency and economy. The introduction of market competition will, it is argued, by stimulating increased provider efficiency, serve both the individual and the collective good:

> a trickle-down effect will ensure that the improved services and increased wealth generated by market competition will benefit all. Relative disparities between the wealthiest and the poorest may widen, but the position of both is raised in absolute terms.
>
> (Bellamy and Greenaway 1995: 475)

Moreover, it is argued, the 'free' nature of health services does nothing to prevent unequal access to health services. State-provided services rather serve only to replace one form of inequality with another. Rationing in the form of price is replaced by the rationing that occurs as a result of the hidden choices of healthcare professionals and managers. Political decisions replace consumer choice and these decisions are subject to political manipulation. Such rationing ultimately serves the interests of providers, not consumers. In contrast to state-provided health services, which deny choice and diminish the possibilities of exit, a market system it is argued enhances the personal choices of individual consumers and their power over the producer. Unlike state services, moreover, which encourage a culture of passivity and dependency, the power to choose between a range of suppliers is seen to enhance the responsibility and self-sufficiency of the health consumer.

## Citizens and consumers

> Citizenship is a status bestowed on those who are full members of a community. All who possess the status are equal with respect to the rights and duties with which the status is endowed.
>
> (Marshall 1950: 87)

A major target of the New Right is the social democratic notion of citizenship and the social and economic rights by which it is typically underpinned. As Clarke (1996: 2) has argued, the citizen is the 'archetypal figure' of the modern welfare state; the two are entwined in a mutually beneficial relationship of rights and duties: 'the citizen is both a precondition of the welfare state and its product'. For New Right theorists, the social and economic rights involved in social democratic notions of citizenship (a right to enjoy good health, for example, or a decent standard of education) are difficult to legitimize and impossible to sustain. They are seen to interfere with individuals' more basic civil rights freely to enter into relationships of contract and exchange and to undermine responsibility and self-reliance. In contrast, the new liberals stress the negative and minimal nature of real rights, defined primarily in terms of the freedom from interference by others, including the state. The operation of these rights, moreover, is to be restricted to the civil and legal, rather than the social or economic spheres. Central to this position is the insistence that there is a difference between the right of individuals to pursue a course of action and their ability to do so. The role of the state is to prevent others from interfering with an individual's freedom to do something, not to provide the material resources which may be necessary for him/her to do that thing. As Plant (1992: 18) has argued, people cannot expect to be able to do all the things that they are free to do: 'The right to life is not the positive right to the means to life'.

The problem with the notion of social rights – to education, housing, health, for example – from the new liberal perspective, is that they are dependent on the provision of resources by the state. Civil and legal rights, by contrast, are identified as real rights because they are believed to be unconditional and absolute. It is argued that they need no resources to underpin them, requiring only that other individuals abstain from certain actions. In this view, for example, there is no limit to the individual's right to be protected from fraudulent exchange or from physical assault by others. Social and political rights are, by contrast, seen as both contestable and ultimately open-ended. There is no common agreement about how they are constituted and it is impossible effectively to define their limits. The fact that social rights involve scarce resources, yet are potentially unlimited, moreover, means that they will of necessity have to be rationed. As such, they cannot by definition be perceived as a right: they cannot be provided equally to all and their achievement by some will be at the expense of others.

The notion of social citizenship, in which rights are underpinned by state-provided resources linked to ideas of social justice, is thus firmly rejected by the New Right. In contrast to what Ignatieff (1989) has called the 'citizenship of entitlement', the citizen of New Right theory is independent of the state. His/her rights and responsibilities derive not from participation in the realm of politics or membership of a community, but from his/her position within the market place and status as taxpayer. In Klein's (1980) extension of the Chicago School's conceptualization, the role of 'Homo economicus' – the 'lonely and self-regarding shopper in the market place' whose rights are constituted via his/her market power and whose consumption in the private realm is characterized by the exercise of choice and the option of exit – supplants that of 'Homo politicus' whose participation in the public realm is marked by the exercise of political 'voice', and whose rights and responsibilities derive from the state: 'a social animal whose habitat is the world of political activity' (Klein 1980: 416).

In this way, the New Right reconfiguration of 'the citizen' serves to deny the possibility of an unanimity of interests on which the notion of the 'public good' depends. The 'public' of the New Right imagination is fragmented into a mass of individual consumers, each seeking to maximize their personal resources and freedom to choose. In particular, in their complaint about the growing burden of state welfare expenditure, the New Right establish a central opposition of interest between the citizen as taxpayer (who may or may not utilize the services paid for) and the citizen as service user (who may or may not have 'paid' for the services he or she receives). A further, and more ideologically loaded, differentiation is made of the latter into those who are seen to be deserving of state support and those who are not – between the respectable poor and the 'undeserving', between the 'scroungers' or the 'work-shy'. From these divisions, and reflecting the replacement of the citizen as political actor by the citizen as economic actor, emerges the new 'rhetorical hero' of New Right ideology, the citizen-consumer:

> In their different ways, the delineation of the taxpayer and the scrounger position the welfare consumer. He (for it remains predominantly 'he and his family') is constructed as responsible and respectable, wishing relief

from the burden of tax in order that he may make wise choices about his and his family's future welfare need and how they are to be met.

(Clarke 1996: 4)

The rise of the 'consumer' as key actor in New Right ideology is exemplified in the 'Citizen's Charters' initiative developed, in the early 1990s, by John Major's Government in the UK. Its aim was to afford those using public services the same rights they would have in the private market: 'The central idea behind it is that citizens, or consumers of state services, shall be equipped with rights which seek to provide substitutes for the right which they would have in the private market. *The Citizen's Charter*, if it is to be effective, must imitate in some sense the rights which people have a consumers in a competitive market' (Pirie 1991: 7).

In line with New Right philosophy, the basis of the 'Charter' approach is that public services must be seen to represent a reworking of the nature of the relationship between the individual and the state, one based not on an individual's 'right' to look to the state for help and support, but on the rights and obligations of a contract based on mutuality and exchange:

> *The Citizen's Charter* represents a radically new approach because it reinforces the idea of public service with the notion of a contract between those who pay for the service and those who provide it. Its assumptions are threefold. They are: that the citizen is entitled to receive some level of service in return for the taxpayers' funds used to finance it; that the citizen is entitled to know what level of service that is; and that he or she is entitled to some form of redress if that level is not obtained.
>
> (Pirie 1991: 8)

## The limits of the market

Critics of the New Right position argue that healthcare is a good example of the only limited extent to which the role of the market-based consumer can be developed within public sector services. They point out that there are considerable constraints on the ability of the consumer of health services to replicate the actions of the consumer in the market. As Shackley and Ryan have argued, the notion of the 'health consumer' assumes certain ideal typical characteristics:

> A good consumer can be defined as someone who can adequately assimilate information on costs and quality of health care, and on the basis of such information, has an ability and a desire to make health care choices and is then prepared to search for the best 'package' of health care in terms of cost and quality.
>
> (Shackley and Ryan 1994: 518)

The consumer of healthcare is unlikely to achieve these characteristics for a range of reasons. Firstly, the consumption of healthcare is typically occasioned by a specific need experienced at a particular point in time. The nature of this need (onset of illness or sudden trauma) is such as that the consumer is unlikely to be in the best position to make active and rational choices; nor will he or she necessarily have the time to consider the relevant information and deliberate between alternative packages of care. The product involved, moreover, is very different from that of other commodities; it is not 'health' that is being purchased, but the means to health (healthcare) and the link between the two is imperfect and unpredictable. There is no guarantee that buying certain forms of care will lead to the desired health gain. Indeed, the peculiar nature of healthcare as a commodity is that the consumer may not be in a position to assess its quality even after it has been delivered. Unlike other goods on the market, moreover, the product cannot be returned and replaced if found to be faulty.

The main problem, however, is that consumers of healthcare, unlike their counterparts in commercial markets, are not typically able to make informed choices about the products they purchase. The average consumer of healthcare is unlikely to possess full information on which to make decisions. Not only may up to date information on which to assess different interventions be unavailable to the general public but even if available may, because of its complex and rarefied nature, be difficult to understand or evaluate. Assessment of the need for, and the relative merits of, different forms of healthcare provision will be dependent on the knowledge and judgements of healthcare professionals. Consumers may want information relating to their health, and explanations about the different forms of healthcare interventions, but may not thereby want, or feel able, to use that information to underpin choice. The relationship between suppliers and consumers of healthcare is thus very different from that of the mutual exchange of the marketplace; not only is the imbalance of information between the two sides considerable, but health consumers typically allow the supplier to make their product choices for them. Indeed, the possibilities of choice may actually be perceived as burdensome to consumers, who may wish to cede the responsibility for decision making to experts. This may not only be due to the large measure of trust they are willing to invest in the professional as supplier but it may also be the result of a desire to avoid 'regret' over unsuccessful outcomes:

> The nature of regret is such that it can only be experienced after a choice has been made. If there is no choice, there can be no regret. By relinquishing the decision-making responsibility to the presumably better informed doctor, the possibility of the patient experiencing regret is eliminated.
>
> (Shackley and Ryan 1994: 531)

Finally, and most importantly, critics of the New Right approach argue that the healthcare market is not a perfect market. There may not be the wide plurality of buyers and sellers that characterizes the self-adjusting commercial market place. If a range of suppliers does exist they may not be located near to the consumer, involving him or her in additional time and other costs to access. There is evidence that, even when information about different suppliers is available (for example, on variations in surgery hours or appointment systems), the public may be disinclined to 'shop around' (Salisbury 1989). Moreover, one of the key characteristics of a perfect market is the absence of 'externalities' such that the factors affecting an individual's utility (satisfaction or welfare) are under his or her control. This condition cannot easily be sustained in the healthcare marketplace in which the choices of one member of the public may affect the health of others or where healthcare interventions may need to be targeted at society as a whole in order to safeguard the health of its individual members. Epidemics provide an obvious example of a situation whereby the lack of take-up of healthcare on the part of individuals (via immunization or vaccination) may endanger the health of others and the wide range of public health regulations covering services such as sanitation and food preparation exemplifies the attempt to protect the individual via measures imposed on the community as a whole. A more dramatic example of the interrelationship between the health of the individual and that of the whole is the growing concern about the global health costs arising from the individual use of antibiotic medicines.

Critics of the New Right position argue that the case of health in this way renders problematic the notion that public services can be effectively provided on the basis of a contract between the individual and the state. There is no guarantee, they point out, that the choices of individuals, pursuing their personal needs and interests, will result in a fair and equitable service. Indeed, just the opposite: such a situation is likely to result in an overall deterioration of the service as individuals making rational economic decisions prove unwilling to invest in the cost of health interventions that are seen to benefit themselves only indirectly or not at all. The problem with the New Right approach, its critics argue, is that it ignores the distinctive character of the public sector which has to combine the interests and concerns of the individual with those of the 'public as the plurality' (the many) and the 'public as collectivity' (the whole) (Ranson and Stewart 1989). The task of the public domain is the provision of 'collective goods': those goods and services which individuals are unable or unwilling to provide themselves – or, indeed, those that they may chose not to receive – but which are nevertheless considered essential for the social health of the nation, literally the 'common-wealth'. The determination of what constitutes a collective good and on what basis it should be provided must be the outcome of collective value judgements rather than the sum of individual choices and informed by considerations of justice and equity as well as by the pressures of competing demands and needs.

Opponents of the new liberalism accept that these judgements or 'collective choices' are not fixed or pre-given, but argue that it is precisely because they require the reconciliation of potentially conflicting needs and demands that they cannot be left to the operation of the market place; they are necessarily political in nature. Politics should not, therefore, be seen as an obstacle to the operation of public agencies – as in the New Right scenario – but rather viewed as integral to or 'constitutive' of them. The political process is the only way in which the conflicting demands, between different individuals and between individuals and the public at large, can hope to be reconciled into some form of consensus or common interest. Indeed, the existence of social rights and obligations underpinned by common values – a social rather than a market contract – is a necessary prerequisite for individuals to exercise the civil rights and freedoms so central to the New Right position. There is only a very limited sense in which an individual is free actively to pursue his or her economic self interests if he or she is hungry, homeless or ill.

## The limits of the state

However, counterpoising the idea of the collective good with that of individual choice in this way may only be to relocate rather than resolve the problem. It begs the central question of how judgements about what constitutes the public good are to be established. The logical extension of the idea of the collective good is that the state, as representative of the people, should make such judgements, but this ignores the possibility that the interests of the officials, politicians and provider groups within the state can be in opposition to those of individual citizens, or that the public in either its individual or collective forms might require better mechanisms to question and confront the decisions that are made on its behalf. The success of the New Right approach, after all, has not only been due to its appeal to individual self-interest but also to the attractiveness of its claims to empower the people against the state. The ideological opposition of the New Right to the role of the state increasingly meshed with the everyday experience of ordinary people, as tenants of council housing, as recipients of state benefits or as residents of state-run residential homes, for example, of services that were patronizing, inflexible and of limited quality. Recasting the citizen as consumer fed into the growing demands of individuals to receive better information about and explanations for the activities of the state bureaucrats and professionals, to be treated with respect and to obtain redress against poor quality or inadequate services. These were attributes which, by and large, were not seen to have been assured by the mechanisms of bureaucratic rationality nor formal democratic representation.

Many of those otherwise critical of the New Right position in this way nevertheless acknowledge the need to recognize the limited ability of the state to speak for 'the people' and the appeal of the greater opportunities for individual choice and control provided by market-based consumerism. The challenge presented by the New Right stimulated the search for new ways of conceptualizing the public sector and the relationship between the individual and the state. The years of the 1980s and 1990s thus saw growing debates about the possibilities of a middle or 'third way' between the extremes of collectivism and consumerism. Such was the emergence of a range of 'new communitarianism' or 'stakeholder' approaches at the political level (Dennis and Halsey 1988; Hutton 1996) as well as academic writing exploring the possibilities of more pluralist forms of welfare provision (Hadley and Hatch 1981; Gilbert and Gilbert 1989) or arguing the need for the development of a new public sector orientation (Stewart and Clarke 1987; Stewart and Walsh 1992). Such positions recognize the importance of greater choice and diversity in public provision, including a key role for private and not-for-profit service providers, but also attempt to reinvigorate the ties of mutual dependence and interest that bind individual citizens together. They set out to balance the 'rights' promised by the new consumerism with the idea of responsibilities (on the part of the public and its representatives) to a broader 'moral community'. Thus Hutton describes the 'stakeholder' idea of 'new Labour':

> It is an explicit statement of the values and principles that had underpinned the century-long attempt to find a just society and moral community that is congruent with private property, the pursuit of the profit motive and decentralised decision-making in markets.
>
> (Hutton 1996)

Central to such attempts is seen to be the importance of reinvigorating the role of 'the public' in policy discourse. Once it had extracted the persona of the consumer, New Right ideology, as we have seen, left very little life in the idea of the public. What remained was captured by the culturally narrow and exclusive concept of 'our people': '. . . the people effectively shrank to the white, law abiding, tax-paying, home-owning, familialized population (and aspirants to it)' (Clarke 1995: 9). In this conceptualization, the public has an essentially passive and largely symbolic political role as silent guard over affronts to populist shibboleths such as 'the British way of life'. Against this process of exclusion and public 'pacification', proponents of the middle way argue that the development of effective public services needs to be based on a more inclusive and active notion of the public which acknowledges the growing diversity of modern society yet is able to provide all its members with a 'stake' or investment in it: 'The unifying idea is inclusion; the individual is a member, a citizen and a potential partner' (Clarke 1995: 9).

Achieving this objective, however, may be more easily said than done. Neither the increased consumer choice of New Right theories nor the local and national forms of representative democracy may be sufficient to the task of reflecting and reconciling the different and potentially opposing interests of citizens, consumers, communities and the public as a whole. Both consumerism and popular democracy are necessary means of representing the public's view, but both may need to be supplemented by the development of new forms and mechanisms for participation which are able to reflect the diversity of the public and acknowledge a citizenry that is 'active but particularized'. The search for the middle ground between the market and the state thus may require the development (or rediscovery) of additional mechanisms for involving the public. Ranson and Stewart, for example, suggest that it may be necessary to consider ways variously of extending the consultative process, encouraging challenges to elected representatives, encompassing public protest and dissent and enabling more active participation in the political process. Moreover, they argue, the responsibility for developing more extensive forms of public involvement must be seen to be part of the role of public organizations; it is their duty, as representatives or servants of the public 'to convene the public discourse . . . to constitute the public as a critical public; to enable the public to be a public' (Ranson and Stewart 1994: 254).

Whether as part of the New Right-driven role of the public service consumer or as part of centre left attempts to rekindle the communal ties and responsibilities of democratic citizens, the issue of public involvement and participation in public sector services was very much on the mainstream political agenda of the 1990s. As the UK approached the 1997 General Election, the future direction of the public sector seemed likely to be shaped by the battle between the contrasting ideals and aspirations of 'shareholder' versus 'stakeholder' capitalism. The following chapters set out to examine the issue of public involvement in the specific context of the UK NHS. Focusing on healthcare purchasing, they will examine the key factors driving public involvement and the nature and implications of the forms it has taken. The potential as well as the limitations of market-based mechanisms will be considered and the possibilities of alternative, more participatory methods will be explored. Before doing so, however, it is necessary briefly to examine the broader structural changes that characterized the development of the UK public sector over the years of the 1980s and early 1990s.

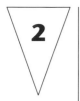

# 2  Restructuring public services

## Introduction

We have argued that the years of the 1980s saw rising international concern about the cost and inefficiency of the social democratic state generally and of its welfare activities in particular. This concern was seen to have led to a widespread reappraisal of the role of the public sector and of the balance between individual and state responsibility. The result, many argue, has been a shift in the boundaries between the public and the private sectors and the global development of new forms of public sector management. This new public management (NPM) is seen to involve the replacement of the traditional bureaucratic paradigm with a new 'post-bureaucratic' paradigm characterized by the adoption of private sector management forms and practices. This chapter examines the nature and extent of the development of NPM in the context of the UK public sector generally and the NHS in particular.

## New public management: new paradigm?

While it is possible to identify common themes and issues underpinning the critique of 'big government', this does not necessarily imply unanimity in terms of the nature of the solution. The notion of a new public management paradigm may serve to over exaggerate the universality of changing forms of contemporary public management within different individual nation-states. The fact that more traditional forms of public administration have generally been eroded does not necessarily mean that they have everywhere been replaced by a single alternative. The specific nature of new ways of organizing and delivering public services, and the extent to which traditional forms have disappeared, is likely to vary considerably from country to country and even, within any one society, from sector to sector. Much will depend on whether individual nation states have either the motive or the opportunity to develop new forms of public sector management and on the very different political contexts and agendas involved (Hood 1995).

Moreover, it is also clear that the precepts and prescriptions of the new public management are themselves lacking in coherence. Most commentators seem agreed that new approaches to public administration typically involve the – possibly uneasy – combination of at least two central strands: the preoccupations of the new 'institutional economics' with competition and choice, on the one hand, and managerialist concerns with the development of professional expertise and the freedom to manage on the other. The particular components of new public managerialism, and the balance between its two central strands, will vary considerably between different societies. In the UK, as in the USA and Australia, public sector development has been characterized by the dominance of business-type managerialism, or what Cutler and Waine (1994) refer to as the 'corporate capitalist' approach. This, it is argued, has produced a pragmatic version of NPM comprising three key elements: tighter political control over expenditure; decentralization of managerial responsibility; and the development of 'neo-Taylorist' managerialist principles. These aim 'to set clear targets, to develop performance indicators to measure the achievement of those targets, and to single out, by means of merit awards, promotion or other awards, those individuals who get "results"' (Pollitt 1990: 56).

Although the emergence of NPM is most commonly associated with New Right administrations, this is not universally the case. Walsh (1995) argues that its rise tends to reflect not so much a left/right divide as a more general political offensive against any government associated with the failure of the state to deliver the promises of the post-war social democratic settlement. As a result, the development of NPM has differed from country to country in terms of the extent to which it has been accompanied by an explicit ideological commitment to privatization. Under left-wing governments in Australia and Sweden, for example, the emphasis has been more on the importance of modernizing the state and improving the quality of its services than on privatization for its own sake. In the UK, however, under the influence of a series of radical conservative administrations, the themes of the new public management have been harnessed more explicitly to a politically inspired drive to privatization. Both have been central features of the wider restructuring of the state that has taken place since the years of the late 1970s. In respect of the organization and delivery of public services, the UK political prescription has been twofold: firstly, wherever possible, state activities and services should be transferred to the commercial or 'not-for-profit' sectors; and secondly, where such transfer is not possible, the efficiency of those services that remain must be

---

Box 2.1    Defining privatization

The concept of privatization is subject to considerable imprecision. Dunleavy (1986: 13) offers a useful initial definition:

> . . . the permanent transferring of service or goods production activities previously carried out by public service bureaucracies to private firms or to other forms of non-public organisation, such as voluntary groups.

This broad definition, however, covers a range of different forms of activity from the transfer of services or assets to the private sector via denationalization (disposal) or the abolition of monopoly status (liberalization), to contracting out the delivery of public sector activities to the private or not-for-profit sectors whilst retaining the public funding and planning of the service. The process of contracting out may not necessarily result in the transference out of state provision; contracts may be placed with in-house or direct labour organizations and, even if placed outside the public sector, may not be so placed permanently. Thus it is important to distinguish contracting out or competitive tendering from the development of the contract relationship *per se*. The latter, where the planning of a service is separated from its delivery and subject to a legally binding agreement of rights and duties, can be developed between bodies which may remain wholly within the public sphere, the function being to increase efficiency by introducing market-type conditions within natural monopolies.

Moreover, whilst both the financing and provision of services/goods may be placed in private hands, the state may nevertheless retain a degree of control over decisions concerning the disposal of assets, for example, via the establishment of regulatory frameworks and/or the retention of a 'golden share'. It is also important to acknowledge the role played by mechanisms other than disposal or contracting out in shifting the balance between the public and private sectors. Thus, a general reduction in public expenditure may, to the extent that it serves to reduce the quality and availability of publicly provided services, act as stimulus to individuals to use private alternatives. The use of financial mechanisms such as tax allowances, direct subsidies and the imposition of charges can also serve to further the development of the non-state sector.

---

improved by subjecting them to the disciplines and practices of the private sector.

## Reforming the UK public sector: a game of two halves

Although some aspects of the process had much earlier origins, the major thrust to the restructuring of the public sector in the UK was provided by the election of a radical Conservative Government in 1979. It was, however, an uneven process which can loosely be divided into two distinct periods or 'waves', the first being from the late 1970s to the mid/late 1980s and the second from the latter years of the 1980s to the present day.

*The first half: contracts, efficiency and economy*

Despite the initial absence of any explicit policy on privatization, the early Conservative administrations effectively undertook the disposal of state assets on a substantial scale, resulting in what one advocate described as '. . . the largest transfer of property since the dissolution of the monasteries under Henry VIII' (Pirie 1985: 21). Apart from the sale of local authority housing (see below), this process of disposal was predominantly concentrated in the industrial and commercial sectors. The form of privatization which characterized developments in the public sector over this period was not disposal but contracting out. Although having a fairly long history, the contracting out of state services has tended to be fairly small scale and focused primarily on those activities too specialist for the state to undertake itself. The early to mid 1980s, however, witnessed an unprecedented increase in contracting out of public sector services. Dunleavy (1986), for example, talks of a 'privatization boom' characterizing this period in which aggressive campaigning on the part of private contractors resonated with the Government's 'firm ideological belief' in the efficacy of the contract mechanism, largely untested, he argues, by empirical investigation (Dunleavy 1986: 15).

There were important differences between local authorities and health authorities in terms of the experience of contracting out over this period. In local government, the growth in competitive tendering was largely generated by Conservative-led local councils ideologically keen, in the face of the 1979 'winter of discontent', to develop contracting as a means of undermining the power of public sector unions. Initially confined to auxiliary services such as street cleaning, refuse collection, school cleaning and school meals, the process was extended by the Local Government Planning and Land Act 1980 to building, construction and maintenance work. In contrast to the predominantly 'bottom-up' development of contracting out in local government, the process in the NHS was imposed 'top-down' by the Government and driven by coercion rather than exhortation. Following the outcome of an 'efficiency scrutiny' of auxiliary services in the Ministry of Defence which was seen to have delivered considerable savings, in 1983 the Government required health authorities to introduce compulsory competitive tendering for their cleaning, catering and laundry services. By the mid 1980s, just under one-quarter of all contracts for auxiliary services had been awarded to the private sector (Butler 1992).

Overall, however, the evidence suggests that the progress of the 'privatization boom' of the early 1980s was uneven and relatively short-lived. It was rather more advanced in central government than in local or health authorities with nearly half of all central agency expenditure on key ancillary services going to the private sector (Ascher 1987). In local authorities, contracting was generally successful only in those areas of work or those councils where in-house services had proved historically unsuccessful. As Ascher (1987: 227) concludes, the sum of local authorities' contracting out activity probably constituted: '... little more than the normal changes in modes of service provision one would expect over time' and by the mid 1980s, some local authorities were returning to in-house provision. The success of contracting out was also limited in the health service where it was adversely affected by its poor timing – immediately following a period of industrial dispute and service reorganization – and by the overtly ideological nature of the initiative, which fostered a more protective stance towards in-house services than might have otherwise been the case. Despite considerable Government pressure, the momentum of contracting in the NHS was seen to have faltered in the face of 'bureaucratic inertia' (Salter 1995: 25).

Other aspects of privatization can be identified within public sector services over this period. The Housing Act 1980 forced the 'disposal' of local authority housing stock by providing sitting tenants with a 'right to buy'; a strategy further encouraged by the increased discounts provided for in the Housing and Planning Act 1986. This legislation also encouraged the process of partnership between local authorities and the private sector in building and refurbishing council properties and by enabling the former to transfer their housing stock to private landlords or Housing Associations. In the personal social services the years of the early 1980s saw a considerable growth in the provision of private residential and nursing care for elderly people, driven by state subsidization. In the period between 1980 and 1986, for example, the volume of private and voluntary homes almost doubled (Johnson 1995).

In education, encouragement of the role of the private sector was provided by the introduction, in the Education Act 1980, of the Assisted Places Scheme, designed to enable state pupils to attend private schools. The promotion of parental 'choice' (in reality, preference) was also furthered by the requirements of the 1980 Act, and the Education Act 1986 served to weaken the role of the local education authority on the governing bodies of schools.

The NHS, of course, has never been a monolithic state service. Since its inception, it has operated in partnership with self-employed professionals (dentists, community pharmacists and general practitioners) and with private suppliers of goods and services (pharmaceutics and hospital supplies). In addition, there has long been the provision for individuals to utilize private insurance schemes to purchase private medical care via private providers or private facilities within the NHS (pay beds). The fully public nature of the service is also compromised by the levying of charges or fees (e.g. prescriptions) which effectively serve as a tax on health. Nevertheless, the years of the early 1980s were marked by a number of policy changes explicitly designed more actively to encourage the role of the private sector within the NHS. The Health Services Act 1980 abolished the Health Service Board which had been established to phase out NHS pay beds. Changes to consultants' contracts were also introduced which enabled them to undertake an increased proportion of their time in private practice. Tax incentives for the purchase of private health insurance were introduced and planning restrictions on the development of private hospitals relaxed. The result was a growth in independent private healthcare provision by 30 per cent in each of the years 1980 and 1981: between 1980 and 1984 there was an overall increase of 50 hospitals providing over 3000 beds. The charge for prescriptions also increased steeply – from 20 pence per item in 1979 to £2.20 in 1987 – and charges for dental and optical consultations were introduced (Johnson 1989).

Despite these initiatives, however, most commentators seem agreed that by the mid 1980s there had been little real change in the overall balance between private and public provision in public sector services. In particular, no move had been made to extend the process of contracting out to the direct provision of health and social care services. As Le Grand and Bartlett (1993: 2) argue, at this time: 'The vast majority of the population was still served by state-funded and state provided systems of education, health care, social services and social security'. Nevertheless, important precedents had been set by these early developments. The significance of competitive tendering, for example, lay less with the financial savings it produced than with the impact it made on the organizational culture of health and local authorities. In particular, it established the principle that the responsibility for purchasing services could be divorced from that for their provision and introduced the idea of provider competition. This principle, as we shall see, was to be developed more dramatically in the later years of the 1980s and early 1990s.

The aim of reducing the role of the public sector was accompanied by a related attempt to improve its operation by the injection of private sector managerial culture. The years of the early 1980s saw a series of reforms with two explicit aims: to improve the economy and efficiency of state provided services and to enhance the freedom of managers to manage those services. In the arena of the central state, the process of reform began with the establishment of an Efficiency Unit, headed by an ex-manager from the Marks & Spencer national retail chain, the then Sir (later Lord) Derek Rayner. The Unit was charged with seeking out waste and advising on ways in which it might be eradicated. Rather than a comprehensive review, the Unit undertook a series of 'scrutinies' of various aspect of the service, undertaken by selected young officials or 'Rayner's raiders' (Massey 1993: 41) and designed to reveal the more general inadequacies of the service.

Although the immediate impact of scrutinies was limited, they provided the motivation for a more extensive onslaught against the perceived inefficiencies of the service in the form of the 1982 Financial Management Initiative (FMI). The FMI involved a review of existing financial and managerial systems based on the now familiar principle of the 'three 'E's' (economy, efficiency and effectiveness) with particular emphasis on the first two. Linked with an initiative to improve the quality of central intelligence on the activities of various departments (the Management Information

System for Ministers or MINIs) the FMI aimed to combine an improved quality of information to 'top management' with the delegation of greater responsibility to middle managers for decentralized budgetary control and performance measurement/appraisal. In the end, the impact of the FMI was limited by a central tension between its managerial and financial aims (House of Commons Committee of Public Accounts 1987: 61) and functioned primarily as a mechanism for greater treasury control of the service.

Despite its limited impact at a central level, a similar approach was taken to the management of the health service at this time. As we have seen, the introduction of competitive tendering aimed to inject some of the ethos of the private sector into the operation of health and local authorities but did little to address what the Government felt to be the core management problems of those services: their costly and inefficient operation. The 1982 enquiry into the management of the health service set out to address these issues. As in the civil service, the enquiry was chaired by an ex-retail businessman, this time from the Sainsbury supermarket chain, Mr (subsequently, Sir) Roy Griffiths. The key problem identified in the report was the lack of overall strategic control of the service, hence its now famous observation that '. . . if Florence Nightingale were carrying her lamp through the corridors of the NHS today, she would almost certainly be searching for the people in charge' (cited in Pollitt *et al.* 1991: 63). Not surprisingly perhaps, the general solution proposed by the small Griffiths team (all businessmen) was that the health service would benefit from the introduction of private sector managerial structures and practice.

The major objective of the subsequent Griffiths reforms was to replace the existing 'consensus management' approach within the service with a 'more thrusting and committed' style of general management (DHSS 1983: 19). The horizontal, multidisciplinary management teams would be replaced by a managerial hierarchy, headed at each operational level (unit, district and region) by a single decision-taker or chief executive. The intended effect of these changes was to introduce a sense of '. . . personal and visible responsibility' (Norman Fowler, quoted in Harrison and Pollitt 1994: 46) on the part of individual managers for setting organizational objectives and assessing the effectiveness with which they are met. Those individuals, moreover, would not necessarily be clinicians, but would possess transferable professional managerial skills and their appointment would be made on the terms and conditions typical of private sector contracts.

The operation of these new style managers was to be underpinned by the development of a range of private sector 'good management' techniques. Rayner-type scrutinies were introduced in 1982 and a programme of annual ministerial reviews of the regional health authorities and regional reviews of the district health authorities was instigated in the following year. To enable comparison of the performance of different authorities, a national performance indicator (PI) package was developed in 1983. This collected statistical information (indicators rather than measures) on a range of aspects of both clinical and non-clinical services as well as manpower, finance and estate management activities. Attempt was also made to improve efficiency by the introduction of private sector resource management techniques and to involve clinical staff in the process. As early as the 1970s, attempts had been made to delegate financial responsibility through consultant-held budgets and the Griffiths Report stimulated further such experiments via the 1983 Management Budgets (MB) initiative. Introduced in 1983 by 'demonstration' in selected health districts, MB was designed to generate greater cost-consciousness on the part of medical and nursing staff by encouraging them to relate workload and service objectives to specific financial allocations. As Harrison and Pollitt argue (1994: 82), the term 'demonstration' was used advisedly, involving as it did: '. . . a straight transfer to the public sector of a technique that had been an integral part of management in the private sector for 40 years.'

The recommendations of the Griffiths Report were based on the twin assumptions of the superiority of private sector managerial forms and of their applicability within the public sector. There was little concern in the Report with the question of the extent to which the proposed style of management would be appropriate to the particular service in question. As Cutler and Waine remark, the key characteristic of the Report was its level of abstraction:

> The reader would learn much more about the views of the authors on management, organisation structure and control than on the substantive issues arising from the services themselves.
>
> (Cutler and Waine 1994: 5)

The transplantation of the tenets of new public managerialism to the NHS, however, was to prove possible to only a very limited extent. Specific initiatives failed to live up to their promise: the PI package, for example, was mainly used in a reactive rather than strategic way and the MB initiative was judged by the Joint Consultants Committee and the NHS Management Board as not '. . . making any worthwhile contribution to the planning and costing of patient care' (cited in Packwood *et al.* 1990). In general, there is evidence of a considerable 'implementation gap' between the recommendations of the Griffiths Report and the operation of the service at a local level: 'The experience of many NHS employees in the years immediately after Griffiths was of lots of top management pronouncements and "initiatives" but little of substance at the level of delivery of services to patients' (Harrison and Pollitt 1994: 48).

In part, this disjunction was due to the realities of implementation; the reforms were top-down and prescriptive, but it was left to individual managers to impose coherence on them at a local level. As a result, the process was largely that of trial and error with an important role being played by the approach of individual managers and by the specific political, historical and organizational contexts of individual authorities. The implementation of NPM techniques, moreover, was not assisted by a general perception of their association with the wider political project of the Government. Many of the proposed changes were seen by local staff as measures to cut staff and expenditure and facilitate the privatization of the service. The general managers in particular were viewed with suspicion: 'as the Government's chosen agents in the imposition of cuts' (Pollitt 1990: 67).

In large part, however, the limited impact of the early management reforms was due to the ability of the medical profession to resist attempts at greater control. The general managers had insufficient power to ensure the subordination of clinicians to organizational objectives and their authority was consistently undermined by the overt and covert influence of these professionals: '. . . doctors retained virtually undiminished their ability to obstruct changes of which they disapprove' (Harrison and Pollitt 1994: 50). As a result, the 'diplomatic approach' to the management of doctors prevailed as general managers tended to focus on implementing the more achievable elements of the reforms or concentrated on responding to more immediate external financial pressures. As one Unit general manager surveyed by Strong and Robinson complained:

> The planning system exists in the NHS simply to legitimise developments that have already taken place . . . One hospital administrator said to me the other day that he was answerable to 96 doctors who were answerable only to God – and four of them didn't even accept that!
>
> (Strong and Robinson 1990: 32)

The reforms did, however, make significant inroads to the autonomy of the nursing profession, effectively demoting the existing nurse-managers to advisory status. Although medicine was the explicit target of the reforms, it was the less powerful nurses who bore the brunt of the attack:

> The power of doctors was too great for an initial assault; too great, indeed even to get a mention in the 1983 management enquiry. Managers moved slowly and had to cover their tracks. But with the nurses it was different. Nursing might be the biggest of the health service trades and the largest single item of health service expenditure, but its influence was weak and its affairs almost unknown outside nursing circles. At a stroke, the 1984 reorganization removed nursing from nursing's own control and placed it firmly under the new general mangers.
>
> (Strong and Robinson 1990: 5)

Although not the major shift in organizational culture anticipated by Griffiths, moreover, as with the development of competitive tendering, some of the initiatives of the first wave of the new managerialism were to lay down important precedents for subsequent, more radical, changes. In addition to greater control over the work of nurses and the professions allied to medicine, the reforms meant that managers had command over some areas of the service, such as bed closures and the deployment of non-medical staff, without the need for the extended consultations characteristic of the 'consensus' managerial approach. In particular, the introduction of mechanisms such as performance review, resource management and cost-improvement programmes introduced a greater cost-awareness into the service, thereby creating a more favourable climate for further shifts to the 'post-bureaucratic' paradigm. Most importantly, perhaps, the establishment of a professional management tier increased the possibility of and potential for increased political control and scrutiny of the service: 'A line of command now stretched out from Whitehall into every branch of the hospital service...' (Strong and Robinson 1990: 26). As these authors argue, the reforms broke once and for all the implicit agreement that doctors should be left to manage their own affairs:

> Where once there had been administration, now there was management from the top to the bottom of the service. The old agreement had been broken. In principle, at least, Whitehall was no longer willing to share power with the clinical trades, no longer content to leave matters to the doctors.
>
> (Strong and Robinson 1990: 27)

### The second half: markets, choice and quality

The late 1980s saw the UK public sector subject to a second more radical wave of privatization. The limited impact of the earlier initiatives prompted the development of different objectives and new forms of their implementation: rather than the pursuit of economy for its own sake, the political emphasis shifted to concerns with 'quality and choice'. In organizational terms, the operation of neo-Taylorist processes was supplemented by the development of 'management by contract' within simulated market conditions. This shift within public sector services thus mirrored that taking place within the private sector from the direct controls of post-Fordist methods to more flexible models of management based on the 'primacy of market-based co-ordination' (Walsh 1995: xiv). Harden (1992: 29) identifies two 'defining features' of the contractual approach: the separation of the responsibility for the policy and planning of a service from the responsibility for its delivery; and the underpinning of this division of functions by an agreed and binding definition of rights and duties. This separation of interests between functional divisions mirrors that of the producer/consumer in the market place.

There are limits, however, to the extent to which the public sector 'market' can emulate the operation of its private sector counterpart. The most important of these results from the fact that the public sector market has to operate within a framework of government funding and regulation. There is a fundamental difference between the allocation of resources through a truly competitive market and through management processes structured as contracts. The former is essentially unplanned, while the latter is (ideally) a means to the more effective planning and coordination of services. In addition, public sector markets may or may not involve competition between providers and these providers may or may not be from outside the state sector. Unlike their commercial counterparts, moreover, the nature and extent of the competition is also 'managed' and the purchasers of a service may not be the direct service users, but organizational or professional agents operating on their behalf. The modified or managed market in this way provides an ideal compromise for a government committed to greater privatization of services but faced with the political unacceptability of their wholesale transference to the private sector. It provides an acceptable form of competition within services which otherwise retain their public funding and thus their susceptibility to central political control.

One of the most dramatic examples of the growth of 'management by contract' occurred at the level of the central state. As FMI ran out of steam, the political perception grew that a more radical restructuring of central state organization was needed. The main rationale for this was the overload on ministers as a result of the excessive size of departments as well as the need to increase incentives for greater economy and quality of service. The proposed solution was to shift from a unitary civil service to a more federal system in which the policy process (deciding what services should be provided) is separated from the executive operations of departments (the delivery of those services) and the latter is performed in semi-autonomous agencies 'hived off' from the central state. The 'Next Steps' agencies so created enjoy considerable operational independence within explicit policy, financial and performance objectives set by the Government.

The separation of functions is designed to enable individual managers to manage more effectively and increase the flexibility and responsiveness of their organizations. It also serves to ensure tighter ministerial control via the quasi-contractual relationship, in which the department becomes the 'customer' of the agency. The pace of this change was considerable: by 1991 over 50 such agencies had been established covering diverse areas of state activity and ranging in size from the smallest, the national weights and measures laboratory, employing 50 staff to the largest, the Social Security Benefits Agency with 68,000 employees (Goldsworthy 1991: 40). The initiative, characterized by one commentator as the '. . . most fundamental restructuring of the British Civil Service since the Northcote–Trevelyan reforms' (Massey 1993: 51), aimed to effect a profound shift in the culture of Whitehall.

The separation of planning and purchasing from the delivery or provision of services also occurred in these years at the level of the local state. In addition to compulsory competitive tendering for a growing range of support services, including white-collar work such as library and computer services, local authorities were increasingly faced with the loss of their core service provision: in housing, education and social services they were required to move from the role of direct provider of services to that of enabler or purchaser of services provided by commercial and 'not-for-profit' agencies: '. . . local authorities' role in the provision of services should be to assess the needs of their area, plan the provision of services and ensure the delivery of those services' (DoE 1991: para 4). The Education Reform Act 1988 further eroded the responsibilities of the local authority by introducing Local Management of Schools (LMS) which enabled schools to 'opt out' from local to centrally funded or 'grant-maintained' status, and by establishing the former polytechnics as independent 'higher education corporations'. In housing services the 'residualization' of the local authorities' provider role, begun by the sale of council houses, was extended by the Housing Act 1988 which enabled tenants to 'transfer out' of council control and gave newly created Housing Action Trusts the management of run-down estates with a view to their eventual disposal to non-statutory sectors. The NHS and Community Care Act 1990 similarly attempted to shift the role of local authority social services departments further away from that of direct provider to purchaser of services and to engender a 'mixed economy' of service suppliers by stimulating the role of the commercial and 'not-for profit' sectors.

It was in the NHS, however, that the simulation of market-type conditions was to prove most advanced. The limited success of the internal management reorganization prompted more radical attempts to restructure the service, culminating in the prescriptions of the NHS and Community Care Act 1990. An internal market was created within the NHS by splitting the service in two: the purchasing side comprised the District Health Authorities (DHAs) and those GP practices willing and large enough to become their own 'fundholders' and the provider side involved the creation of independent self-managing units or Trusts. Unlike the organization of social care services, which was driven by the explicit aim of reducing the role of public sector provision, the NHS reforms involved the retention of existing providers, although private organizations were able to bid for purchaser contracts and some attempt was made to enhance the role of private health insurers and service providers. To an extent, therefore, the reforms represented an attempt to expand and organize more systematically the pre-existing practice of DHAs trading services between themselves.

The new provider Trusts, while not independent legal entities, nevertheless were given considerable operational and financial autonomy. Managed by a board of directors, including NHS clinical and administrative staff as well as laypersons with managerial experience, the Trusts were effectively to operate as self-managing businesses, responsible for the management of both 'inputs' (staff, property, facilities) and 'outputs' in terms of services provided. These latter were to be developed on the basis of contracts with a range of purchasers from within and, increasingly, outside their original authority. Contracts, obtained in competition with other provider units, would specify broad performance and quality targets as well as appropriate fee structures. Funded on the basis of population characteristics rather than on previous delivery patterns, purchasers were charged with developing a strategic overview of the services needed for the health of their local populations, under the broad direction of the newly established central NHS management executive.

Despite the radical nature of the proposed changes, the aim was that the service should be characterized initially by a 'steady-state' situation in which health authorities continued to buy from existing suppliers and the majority of provider units remained directly managed. This situation continued until the third wave of the reforms in 1992. The development of GP fund-holding was similarly halting; with the first wave of fundholding involving only around 300 practices (Kendall and Moon 1994). The third year of the reforms however, assisted by a series of policy adjustments (such as the reduction in the 'qualifying' list size for fundholding status), saw the end of this steady state: 1993 witnessed a dramatic growth in the number of both independent Trusts and GP fundholders. The year was also marked by the 'unfettering of purchasers' (p. 172) as they moved away from historic patterns of contracting. The development of more strategic purchasing to achieve greater cost-effectiveness eroded traditional purchaser–provider alliances and increased the complexity and sophistication of the contracting process (Appleby 1994). The progress of organizational change, moreover, continued, characterized by the merging or closer cooperation of some health authorities, the development of forms of smaller scale, locality purchasing by others and by the incorporation of the regional health authorities into the civil service structure of the NHS.

There is evidence that, as a result of these organizational changes, the public–private boundary within the NHS shifted significantly. In addition to the continued growth in charges for specific services, (prescriptions, dentistry, eye tests) the Health and Medicines Act 1988 freed providers to charge commercially profitable rates for NHS pay beds. In 1994, the *Health Service Journal* reported a keen interest on the part of private insurance companies in this facility with the Norwich Union for one having established contracts with some 68 Trust hospitals. The impact of the Private Finance Initiative further encouraged proposals for public–private sector collaboration, not just in the design, building and finance of healthcare facilities, but also increasingly in the provision of clinical services. The rise in the purchase of private residential services and, via GP fundholding, of private hospital services are also examples of the increasing crossover between public and private healthcare which occurred during the late 1980s and early 1990s. In addition, many have commented on a more general process within the NHS of redefining the boundaries of healthcare which has reduced the comprehensiveness of health provision and 'encouraged' individuals to utilize private sector alternatives. This approach involves paring down healthcare to acute services only and redefining as social care (and thus potentially as means testable) non-acute and continuing care arrangements: '. . . stripping down to a leaner acute/curative clinical model of hospital treatment and the shedding of continuing and non-acute care which are then redefined as social care to which one does not have the right of access on a free at the point of delivery basis' (Vickridge 1995: 77). This process has particularly affected elderly people as rehabilitation units and continuing care beds have been closed without the provision of community-based alternatives. Vickridge (1995) cites examples of elderly patients being discharged prematurely from hospital beds into nursing homes and individuals refused access to accident and emergency departments and diverted, without proper medical investigation, to residential care.

It is clear that in these and many other ways the foothold of the private sector in the NHS and other areas of state activity, such as housing and the personal social services, is increasingly secure and that its expansion may be a matter of time and/or greater national economic prosperity (Johnson 1995). It is clear too that the shifting boundary between the public and the private spheres is underpinned by an increased political acceptance of the inevitability, even desirability, of a more 'mixed economy' of provision. Thus a policy document produced by the 'new Labour' opposition in 1994 focused on the ways in which more private–public partnerships could be encouraged and Chris Smith, as the then Shadow Social Security Secretary commented on the importance of lowering the public's expectation of what the state can provide:

> Some argue that it is only the state that can possibly deliver all the elements of proper social security. I disagree. Of course there are some things that only the state can do. But the principle must surely be that the state acts as the guarantor of all provision, the regulator of all provision – and the administrator of some. The welfare state is after all a framework which the government sets in order to enable citizens to achieve security; it is not a particular mechanism *per se* for delivering that security.
>
> (Chris Smith, *The Guardian* 8 May 1996)

The shifting ideological positions of politicians in respect of the public–private divide, moreover, appear to be reflected in the views of the public as a whole. Public attitude surveys undertaken in the early 1990s indicated a '. . . strong current of support for allowing people to choose between the state and the private market . . . The better off value state provision, but they wish to be able to complement it from the private sector' (Taylor-Gooby 1991: 13). Moreover, while the changes within the NHS and other public services may not have been sufficient to shift the balance disproportionately in favour of the private sector, they have nevertheless significantly altered the face of public sector organizations. The growth of management by contract and the simulation of market-like conditions within the public sector have, possibly irreversibly, changed the way in which its services are organized and delivered. It is to the implications of these changes for the relationship between the state service sector and the public as citizens, consumers and local communities, that Chapter 3 now turns.

# 3 Politics, markets and accountability

## Introduction

The drive for privatization and the growth of the new public managerialism resulted, as we have seen, in significant changes in the organization and delivery of public sector services. The separation of policy making from the administration of services, the blurring of the boundaries between public and private organizations and the increased dominance of contract and market mechanisms, resulted in more fragmented and diverse service structures. In this chapter, we consider the nature of these changes in more detail and their implications for the rights and responsibilities of the public (both as citizens and as service users) in respect of state services as well as for the accountability of those who purchase or provide these services.

## The fragmented state

The result of the increased privatization and decentralization of the state services that occurred in the UK during the 1980s and 1990s has been the emergence of a growing number of agencies operating somewhere between central and local state and between public and private spheres. These 'intermediate bodies' comprise a range of different types of organizations with a variety of functions. Their categorization is not assisted by the changing terminology of political analysts and/or, some would argue, a policy of deliberate confusion on the part of central government. It is possible, however, to differentiate three broad tiers of what has been described as the 'vast archipelago of the government's non-elected executive, administrative and advisory machinery' (Dynes and Walker 1995: 130).

---

**Box 3.1   The fragmented state**

**The inner ring**

In addition to the central government departments themselves, the first, or 'inner ring' comprises the executive arm of the central policy departments – the quasi-autonomous 'Next Steps' agencies. Examples of these agencies include the Social Security Benefits Agency, the National Health Service Estates and the Training and Employment Agency.

**The periphery**

The second tier involves the 'traditional quangos' (quasi-autonomous non-governmental bodies), subsequently referred to as non-departmental public bodies (NDPBs). Defined by the Cabinet Office as the 'adjuncts to government', these comprise three different types: tribunals covering formal processes such as Social Security Appeals, advisory bodies on an extremely diverse range of matters such as the 'Consultative Committee on Badgers' and the 'Welsh Office Place Names Advisory Committee' and executive agencies such as the Commission for Racial Equality or the Housing Corporation. The regional arms of central government departments, such as the Urban Development Corporations, the Integrated Regional Offices and the 'outposts' of the NHS Executive are also included in the peripheral state category.

**The outer periphery**

The final tier of state activity comprises the new state agencies or 'new quangos'. These are not directly part of the state and have typically resulted from the increased role of the private sector and/or the reduced responsibilities of local authorities. The agencies of the new state include both predominantly public bodies such as the NHS Trusts/Commissions or the Funding Agency for Schools, as well as private or not-for-profit agencies like the Housing Associations and Housing Action Trusts, the Training and Employment Councils and the governing bodies of state schools.

---

Despite explicit intentions to reduce the size of the central state and constrain the proliferation of quangos, the Conservative governments of both Margaret Thatcher and John Major presided over a steady rise in their number. A 'Democratic Audit' undertaken in the early 1980s identified over 5500 such bodies, the great majority of which were operating at a local level (Marr 1995). The growth of these new intermediate bodies has been largely incremental and ad hoc, lacking any overall guiding principles or philosophy. As a result, the nature of their relationship to central and local government is, in many cases, ambiguous. In particular, despite the fact that their operation has considerable autonomy, the development of these agencies has been characterized by the absence of any consistent approach to the issues of constitutional or legal accountability.

## The modernization of accountability

The precise meaning of the term 'accountability' is difficult to pin down. As Day and Klein (1987) point out, the dictionary definitions of accountability are testimony to the shifting and multifaceted nature of the concept: 'To account is to answer for the discharge of a duty or for conduct. It is to provide a reckoning. It is to give a satisfactory reason for or to explain. It is to acknowledge responsibility for one's actions' (Day and Klein 1987: 5). At its most basic, political 'accountability' is the process which provides the link between those who govern and those on whose behalf they do so. It is a dual process, involving those to whom the public grants authority not only being required to 'give account' of their actions and activities, but also being 'held to account' by that public. The exercise of accountability would seem to involve three central preconditions. The first is that of transparency. Effective accountability requires that those who govern are visible and that information about their actions is available to the public. Its exercise therefore requires the promotion of full and informed debate and an open decision-making process: '... accountable government can only flourish on openness that seeks continually to inform the public and promote knowledgeable discourse' (Ranson and Stewart 1989: 18).

Secondly, the process of accountability involves not just the *right* of people to call those in power to account, and the responsibility of the powerful to give account of their actions, it also crucially depends on the *ability* of those who are governed to call their decision makers to account. Effective accountability thus requires that those without power are able to exercise some form of control over those who rule on their behalf. This may range from the fairly blunt and unwieldy mechanism of periodic elections to more specific and immediate processes such as audit, complaint or inspection. Finally, the concept of accountability also assumes the condition of indivisibility. To be able to hold its representatives, or public agencies, to account the public must know where the responsibility for decision making lies. The chain of organizational command must therefore lead in a clear and visible way to a single individual who carries the ultimate responsibility. As J.S. Mill (1962: 332) argued: '... there must be one person who receives the whole praise of what is well done, the whole blame of what is ill.'

The traditional public sector organization is based on the assumptions of Weberian bureaucratic rationality in which upward accountability to the government of the day, and through it to the community of citizens, is ensured by the execution of politically agreed objectives by a body of salaried permanent officials. These officials or 'civil servants' are subject to continuous supervision within a formal administrative hierarchy and are accountable to the national executive (government), which is in turn subordinate and accountable to the legislature (Parliament). As well as their responsibility to the government of the day, the traditional civil servant is also to serve as a 'neutral guardian' of the rights of the people, ensuring that government is seen to be operating in the wider public interest. The particular promise of bureaucracy is to transcend narrow sectional interests: '. . . to insulate the administration of the public realm from political and personal "passions"' (Clarke 1995: 4).

The greater size and complexity of the modern state, however, has witnessed the emergence of additional – and possibly conflicting – lines of accountability. Most obviously perhaps, with the evolution of the service state, the bureaucrats are joined by another key group – that of the 'expert' or the professional – which claims its authority not from delegated political responsibility but from the possession of specialist knowledge and skills. The accountability of professionals is thus to their peers, not to the public via the elected government. They share with the civil servants, however, the commitment to override their personal interests in the pursuit of the public good. For writers such as Marshall, the professionals' sense of responsibility to the standards and duties of their profession was seen to be vital to ensuring the accountability of the public sector (Marshall 1965). Others, such as Day and Klein (1987), argue that there are central tensions between the lines of professional and political accountability. What they term the 'growing army' of experts represents in their view a new tier in the hierarchy of administration which cuts across and potentially conflicts with the lines of political accountability, providing 'dead ends, instead of links in the chain of accountability' (Day and Klein 1987: 224).

More recent years have seen the development of further forms or layers of accountability. The separation of policy and administrative tiers encouraged by the new public management results in a concomitant separation of political and managerial lines of accountability. In contrast to political accountability which involves decisions about what is to be done (ends), managerial accountability carries responsibility for decisions about the way in which things should be done (means). The latter may also involve delegated authority for the effective conduct of a range of specific tasks or functions which may introduce additional lines of financial accountability, process accountability (efficiency) and/or programme accountability (effectiveness). With these new arrangements, the prescriptive rules and directives of traditional bureaucratic forms of control are replaced by specific and detailed controls over individuals' performance. The accountability of those given delegated responsibility is ensured by the imposition of a range of explicit targets and standards which are used to scrutinize and assess their performance. The mechanisms of political and bureaucratic accountability thus give way to those of the 'contract accountability' of market relationships.

For the proponents of the new public management, who consider that the operation of traditional bureaucracies is characterized by ministerial overload, the separation of political and financial/administrative accountability is perceived to be a superior arrangement; freeing managers to manage and releasing ministers from the responsibility for the day-to-day operation of their departments: 'Ministers must be accountable to Parliament and to the public for the spending of . . . huge sums of money. Such accountability does not mean that Ministers should be involved in operational decisions. On the contrary, these decisions must be taken locally by operational units' (Cabinet Office 1988). The separation of policy and administrative levels is seen not only to improve the efficiency and economy of these agencies' operation but also, insofar as these measures of performance are publicly accessible, increase their susceptibility to external scrutiny. Moreover, it is argued, the focus of the new agencies is more restricted, making it easier to identify exactly who is responsible for what. As a senior member of the National Audit Office commented on the 'Next Steps' initiative:

> What we're getting in agencies are areas of activity in a way being ring-fenced, being more readily identifiable from within the department; being required to set performance measures, targets, being required to produce an annual report and accounts. So therefore some elements have become more readily visible.
>
> (Quoted in Massey 1993: 68)

In addition to strengthening 'arm's length' accountability via regulatory and contract mechanisms, the restructuring of the public sector will, it is argued, facilitate the more direct accountability of agencies to their consumers or clients. In contrast to the unwieldy and unspecific 'community of citizens' of traditional forms of political accountability, the new public management establishes a new, strengthened, role for members of the public as individual users of particular services. The introduction of market systems into the public sector is designed to give the consumer of public services the same rights as those of the customer of a private firms, these rights being underpinned by the possibility of choice between competing providers. This, its proponents contend, provides for a more direct form of public accountability than that available via the indirect control of the ballot box. As one Conservative Cabinet Minister argued, the 'key point' about public services is not whether the people who run them are elected, but:

> whether they are producer-responsive or consumer-responsive. Services are not necessarily made responsive to the public simply by giving citizens a democratic voice, and a distant one at that, in their make-up.
>
> (William Waldegrave cited in Walsh 1995: xv)

As we have seen, a major vehicle for the new role of the 'customer-citizen' was the introduction, in the early 1990s, of the Citizen's Charters. Reflecting the themes of the new public management – quality, choice, performance and value for money – the Charters were explicitly designed to improve the direct accountability of public services to the individual consumer: 'to make public services answer better to the wishes of their users . . .' (Prime Minister's Office 1991: 2). Providers of services such as education, health, transport, etc. are required to provide regular public information about the performance of their agencies. The greater transparency of public agencies will, it is argued, enable consumers to compare their performance with other like agencies and to exercise their preference between them: 'Targets should be published together with full and audited information on the results achieved. Whenever possible, information should be in comparable form, so there is pressure to emulate the best' (p. 5).

In the NHS, for example, *The Patient's Charter* of 1991 set out a number of standard entitlements for those using health services. These ranged from the general right of individuals to receive care on the basis of health need rather than ability to pay to the much more specific 'right' to be admitted for treatment no more than two years after being placed on the waiting list. The statement of entitlements was accompanied by a detailed list of service standards to be met by providers, covering issues such as waiting times for ambulance services and outpatient appointments. The publication of *The Patient's Charter* was followed by the circulation of a national Performance Guide (NHSE 1994) enabling comparison of the relative success of individual health authorities in achieving the standards set out in the Charter and designed to enable consumers to make more informed decisions about their healthcare.

As we have indicated, the Citizen's Charters initiative was part of a more general process of transforming the citizen qua political actor into the citizen as consumer. The entitlements of the Charter were conceived as the contractual rights accruing to the individual within the market rather than those which derive from that individual's membership of a community: the right to individual choice, for example, rather than to collective security; to be consulted about rather than to participate; to pursue 'exit' rather than to utilize 'voice'. In contrast to the substantive nature of citizen rights, however, the 'rights' of the consumer enshrined in the various Charters were largely procedural. While they imposed a limited range of duties and constraints on those providing services and opened up their performance to the scrutiny of local purchasers and central government, they did not afford individual consumers any direct sanctions over those who fail to achieve their standards. There was little attention generally given to ways in which the entitlements could be enforced, nor acknowledgement that their achievement may require the diminution of the power of others. Thus, within the first *Patient's Charter* in 1991, for example, we find the right of patients to seek a second opinion was rendered largely meaningless by the fact that GPs remained in a position to prevent them from doing so. The mechanisms for ensuring accountability to consumers, such as market surveys or consumer feedback, moreover, were those of the private firm rather than the democratic process and as such arguably more a management tool than a means of enhancing the power of service users. As Klein concludes, overall the impact of *The Patient's Charter* can be seen to be largely symbolic, introducing '. . . a new rhetoric and set of expectations in the NHS, marking precisely the kind of shift of power from providers to consumers envisaged in the Griffiths' report' (Klein 1995: 212).

## Eroding the political checks and balances

The increased emphasis on new 'managerialist' forms of accountability was accompanied over the years of the late 1980s and early 1990s by gradual erosion of the role of more traditional forms of popular democratic accountability, particularly at a local level. As we have seen, the restructuring of public services was promoted as a politically neutral process, designed only to improve organizational efficiency and to develop more flexible mechanisms for financial and managerial accountability. Many have argued, however, that the changes have considerable implications for the existence of the traditional checks and balances of the democratic process. The first casualty may be the condition of indivisibility. The greater complexity and fragmentation of the state may mean it is difficult to identify exactly who is responsible for what, making it impossible to call to account and apportion blame when things go wrong. Thus was the situation in the former Wessex Regional Health Authority in the late 1980s which was criticized by external auditors for the mismanagement of public funds in the development of its information systems plan (RISP). The lack of any effective response to these criticisms, and the subsequent squandering of large sums of public money, resulted from the confusion between the NHS Executive, the WRHA board and senior managers of the authority over precisely where the responsibility for the problem rested.

The practical and conceptual difficulties of separating the spheres of policy generation and administration, moreover, may provide considerable potential for an intentional blurring of the lines of accountability, enabling politicians to place responsibility for the effects of their policies on those charged with their implementation. Thus, the very public battle that took place at the beginning of 1996 between the sacked director of the prison service, Derek Lewis, and the then Home Secretary Michael Howard over who should be held to account for failures in prison security. Claiming that he was sacked to 'save the skin' of the Home Secretary, Lewis argued on BBC television that the separation of policy and administrative responsibilities was 'a political fig leaf' ('Newsnight' 29 March 1996). In the same way, identifying what he perceived as an emerging culture of 'anxiety, blame and risk avoidance' within the civil service resulting from the NPM agenda, a former Home Office deputy secretary placed the blame on 'Politically convenient but obscure distinctions between policy and operations – and between accountability and responsibility' (Faulkner quoted in Ghazi and Bevins 1996).

The separation of policy and administration may also serve to undermine the precondition of transparency. The relative autonomy of agencies such as the 'Next Steps' may, in providing greater freedom of action for their chief executives, potentially weaken the opportunities for detailed parliamentary scrutiny of their activities (Flynn *et al.* 1990). The proliferation of tiers of delegated or contracted organizational activity may worsen this situation insofar as it extends the distance between policy development and its delivery. Thus the National Audit Office expressed its concern about the operation of semi-private agencies such as the Training and Enter-prise Councils (TECs): 'the department itself would become one stage further removed from the monitoring agents, leaving [them] with monitoring responsibilities that the department, itself not in a position to demonstrate effective scrutiny and control procedures, was supposed to ensure were in place' (1989, cited in Doig 1995: 205). Such problems may be further exacerbated in a more privatized and entrepreneurial culture, where the pressures of competition and profit-making may militate against a proper regard for the normal constitutional and legal procedures of open govern-ment. Claims of 'commercial confidentiality' may provide a convenient defence against the inquisitiveness of the public.

Formal parliamentary scrutiny (of both executive and administration) is provided by the Committee of Public Accounts (PAC), other select com-mittees and by the National Audit Office (NAO) for the NDPBs and by the Audit Commission for local and health authorities. The Audit Act 1983 gave the latter two bodies greater powers to undertake external reviews and surveys of, as well as to stimulate more coherent audit processes within, the various intermediate agencies. The evidence suggests, however, that the impact of such bodies may be limited. Both the NAO and the PAC have publicly expressed concerns about the effectiveness of accountability proced-ures and in particular about their access to full information on the accounts and activities of 'hived-off' agencies (PAC 1993–4). The impact of the select committee system may be similarly restricted: 'Suffering from inadequate resources, integration into the decision-making process, and ministerial disregard for their reports' (Doig 1995: 198). Doig concludes that the problem arises from the mixed messages emanating from the centre about the appropriate balance to be obtained between the operational autonomy of the agencies on the one hand and the requirements of public probity on the other.

Paralleling the loss of parliamentary scrutiny at a national level, many commentators on the new public management have expressed concern over what Walsh (1995) has termed the 'erosion of the middle'; the diminution of the 'countervailing power' of local electorates/governments. The result of the local delegation of central state activities and the loss of functions from local authorities, some fear, has been the creation of a 'new magistracy' (Stewart 1992); an unelected tier of local government freed from political control or scrutiny at a local level. Although it is important to acknowledge the limitations of electoral accountability, nevertheless the local and visible role of elected members enhances the possibility of their being held and/or called to account for their actions. Unlike local councillors, the members of these intermediate bodies are unelected, may conduct their business in secret and may not be subject to the penalties of surcharge and disquali-fication nor to the revocation of their mandate via the local electorate.

Research undertaken by Weir in 1994 revealed that only one third of these bodies was accountable to either of the main auditing bodies (the NAO or the Audit Commission), only 14 per cent were covered by an ombudsman and only 2 per cent were covered by 'open government' codes (cited in Marr 1995: 80). As Marr comments, the result has been a 'quiet and anti-democratic revolution':

> Up and down the country, week after week, in the administrative offices of hospitals, in schools, in local business centres, in their own premises and in private houses, thousands of people gather privately to spend our money . . . their names are unknown to the wider public, their views and arguments are unreported and their stewardship is opaque. There is no central list of this administrative class.
>
> (Marr 1995: 85)

At the same time as providing agencies with greater freedom from popular or parliamentary scrutiny at local or national level, critics of the new public management argue that it must also be seen to increase the susceptibility of those agencies to ministerial or cabinet direction. The reform of the public sector, they argue, has been a twin-sided process in which the decentralization of responsibility has been accompanied by a tighter and more centralized line of political control (Pollitt 1990). The key vehicle for this control is that of the newly created managerial tier which, increasingly subject to fixed-term appointments and performance assessment, is likely to be less resistant to political direction than is the traditional bureaucrat:

> The New Right politicians will pursue managerialism as a method of controlling bureaucracies and implementing the cultural changes defined by their ideology of neo-liberal/conservatism. They are 'licensing' it, imbuing managers with elite status because they see them as powerful allies'.
>
> (Massey 1993: 28)

As well as a means of controlling the bureaucracy, the encouragement of private sector managerialist approaches within the public services was also designed to counteract the perceived power of professional and producer groups to further their own interests at the expense of those of the consumers. This counterpoising of the professional/public interest was made most explicit by the then Prime Minister, John Major:

> The changes we are making in the public services may not always appeal much to the unions and professional bodies. But they should be very attractive to individuals and that attractiveness is important if the public services are to compete in an increasingly active and tight labour market.
>
> (Cited in Stewart and Walsh 1992: 508)

Mechanisms such as the Citizen's Charters, for example, have been explicitly promoted as a means of confronting the entrenched power of the professional with the new found authority of the citizen-consumer. This is made very clear in the White Paper on *The Citizen's Charter*:

> Professional inspectorates can easily become part of a closed professional world. *The Citizen's Charter* will therefore begin to open up inspectorates to the outside world. It will make them more responsive to public concerns.
>
> (Prime Minister's Office 1991: 40)

Other mechanisms associated with NPM such as career restructuring and deskilling, the imposition of performance measures and performance-related pay and management by contract may, by increasing the transparency of professional activity, also serve to heighten its susceptibility to increased managerial control. Even within the NHS, the home of some of the most powerful and entrenched professionals, there is evidence, as we have seen, that the years of the late 1980s and early 1990s saw some inroads into professional control. The main effect of the growth of public sector markets may thus have been not to enhance the power of the consumer-citizen as much as to shift control from one group of professionals to another: from the professional provider to the professional manager.

## Accountability in the NHS

The tension between centralized control and local accountability – 'between seeing members of health authorities as agents of central government' on the one hand and as 'autonomous actors with responsibilities of their own' on the other (Day and Klein 1987: 76) – has long been characteristic of the NHS and provides a 'constant theme' in the successive reorganizations of the service. At its inception, a highly centralized management structure was combined with the expectation that health authorities would also identify and respond to the needs of their local populations (Klein 1990b). The NHS Reorganisation Act 1972 established a more explicitly managerial role for the new area health authorities, arguing that they were too large effectively to perform a representative function. The expression of local opinion was to be provided by the newly established Community Health Councils (CHCs). These bodies combined democratic and market-based approaches to public involvement, being designed to represent both the views of specific groups of health consumers as well as the interest of the community at large (see Chapter 5 for a more detailed discussion of the CHCs).

   In the event, the attempt to shift the balance towards central control and direction was largely unsuccessful. In particular, the assumption that the more narrowly defined and constituted area health authorities would represent more effective links in the line of accountability between the centre and the periphery proved unfounded. The limited time and expertise of members rendered them unable to understand the complexity of the service and the system of consensus decision making at a local level proved resistant to their attempts at control. The subsequent reform of the service in 1982 was thus characterized by a simplified organizational structure and by a renewed emphasis on decentralization and local autonomy. The operation of the newly created District Health Authorities was to be characterized by local level decision-taking 'with the minimum of interference by any central authority, whether at the region or in central government departments' (DHSS 1979). Even here, however, the central tension between local and central control remained as the appointment of the chairpersons of the new District Health Authorities was to be subject to greater government scrutiny and the representation of the local authorities and producer groups was reduced. Moreover, the local autonomy of the service remained subject to the constraints of central funding.

The recommendations of the Griffiths Report in the early 1980s, as we have seen in Chapter 2, attempted to enhance central control by the introduction of a single-tier general management structure leading directly from regional, local and unit level to the Secretary of State. This process was given a final shift in the 1990 reforms of the NHS which further strengthened the central chain of political command and removed local authority and trades union representatives from the new business-style management boards. These boards were not required to meet in public, nor make the proceedings of their meetings publicly accessible. As Klein comments:

> The 1989 model looks like achieving what the 1974 reorganisation failed to do, which is to turn health authorities into boards of directors. There is to be no direct representation, whether of the producer or the consumer interests. It is the managers who are to be seen as proxy consumers.
>
> (Klein 1990a: 26)

The susceptibility of health authorities/trusts to central political control, moreover, was increased by the manner in which their non-executive members were appointed. The chairs of both provider and purchaser bodies were appointed by the Secretary of State for Health and the remaining members appointed by what has been described as 'a complex sequence of word-of mouth, personal recommendation and vetting' (Marr 1995: 87). The evidence suggests that this provided considerable room for the operation of political patronage. Thus Marr (1995) cites the case of one NHS Trust whose five newly appointed members included the wife of the local Tory MP, a retired Tory councillor, the former Conservative leader of district council and the chair of the local Conservative Association. The perception of political bias is reinforced by the now famous quote of Baroness Denton in 1993 concerning the process of appointment:

> You don't put in people who are in conflict with what you are trying to achieve. It's no good going on an NHS Trust if you don't believe in the policy that the Department of Health is pursuing.
>
> (Cited in Marr 1995: 87)

The fate of the Community Health Councils following the 1990 reforms may be seen as evidence of a political desire to constrain potentially 'oppositional' public involvement at a local level. Despite expectations that the reforms would enhance the role of the councils, a series of government circulars and guidelines subsequent to the 1990 Act effectively served to limit their operation in a range of ways. Councils were given no rights in respect of GP fundholding practices or non-NHS premises and their right to attend meetings of the boards of NHS Trusts and Health Authorities was reduced (Lupton *et al.* 1995). Leaked documents from the Department of Health suggest this situation may have resulted from anxiety on the part of both managers and the Government about what was seen to be the potentially political nature of the councils. Concern was expressed about the extent to which the 'legitimate' activity of critical comment '. . . shades into direct political action against the government of the day' (Jobling 1990: 278). Whilst appearing to confirm the right of CHCs to maintain an independent view, this document nevertheless advised that the councils would have to show that they were able to work collaboratively with their local health authorities if they were to have an effective role in the new NHS marketplace: 'The CHC would have to demonstrate that it was prepared to work with and not against management' (ibid.). The result of this approach, from the perspective of the councils at least, was effectively to subject their operation to the 'grace and favour' of local NHS managers.

The organizational devolution of the service has thus not been accompanied by increased local political control and accountability. The strengthening of mechanisms for upward political and financial control, however, has introduced new organizational tensions. Two aspects of this are worth noting. The first results from the extent to which the erosion of local accountability increases the strain placed on the lines of centralized accountability. This problem is exacerbated by the greater number and complexity of the semi-autonomous agencies created by the market reforms. The result it is argued may be an 'accountability overload' as the mechanisms of central political and managerial accountability prove insufficient to the task:

> A burden is being put on the accountability of ministers that it is probably beyond their capacity to bear. It is difficult enough to expect ministers to accept responsibility for the acts of civil servants who are directly under their control, without expecting them to extend their responsibilities as is required by the erosion of accountability at a local level. It is likely that the increasing burden of accountability on ministers will not be matched by an acceptance of responsibilities.
>
> (Stewart *et al.* 1992: 8)

We have already noted examples of the way in which the separation of policy and administration has served to inhibit the acceptance of responsibility for service failure and of the only limited extent to which the mechanisms of 'contract accountability' have functioned to ensure adequate standards of conduct within the operation of public agencies. In this context it is interesting to find that, in 1993, the Audit Commission (1993: 1) was moved to complain that 'fraud and corruption and the stewardship of private and public sector accounts have never had a higher profile'.

The second area of tension arises from the political difficulties of reconciling central and local demands. The day-to-day and visible responsibility for implementing the Government's policy decisions falls to local managers. It is they, rather than the officials in government departments or the NHSE, who face the difficult task of reconciling competing demands and justifying the resulting shape of the service. Such a task becomes particularly critical in a context where increased demand but finite resources requires managers to make decisions about the prioritization or 'rationing' of services. Establishing local support for (or at least acceptance of) such decisions, however, is made more difficult as the extent of public participation in or control over the service is reduced. There is some evidence that, as a result, purchasers may be increasingly constrained in their decision-taking by perceptions of a 'democratic deficit' (Redmayne 1992). Attempts to achieve legitimacy in the eyes of their local populations, however, may present purchasers with an alternative and potentially conflicting set of imperatives to those emanating from central government.

Partly in response to this dilemma, government guidelines subsequent to the 1991 reforms have begun to stress the responsibility of healthcare purchasers to involve local people more actively in their decision making. In place of the formal representation of local interests, health authorities are themselves to cultivate the role of 'champion of the people', and seek out new ways of involving and consulting local people. This involvement, moreover, is to be extensive and ongoing: '[The aim] should be to involve local people at appropriate stages throughout the purchasing cycle: a combination of information-giving, dialogue, consultation and participation in decision-making and feedback rather than a one-off consultation exercise' (NHSME 1992: 3–4). The responsibility to develop a more active relationship with the public moreover applies to GP as well as health authority purchasers. Guidelines for GP fundholders issued in 1994, for example, in addition to emphasizing the need to establish mechanisms for managerial, professional and financial accountability also stress the importance of accountability to patients and the wider public through involvement in 'service planning and review' as well as publishing information and monitoring complaints (NHSE 1994).

Research indicates that health purchasers are, to varying degrees and in varying ways, attempting to develop these responsibilities. Although still patchy and largely ad hoc, public involvement is nevertheless increasingly on the agenda of most health authorities. Its specific forms and extent are discussed in subsequent chapters. The ability of purchasers to extend public participation, however, will depend on the extent to which they are able to reconcile the demands for increased local responsiveness with those of strengthened central scrutiny and to manage the more general 'crisis of accountability' that may increasingly come to characterize the service.

# 4 Understanding public involvement

## Introduction

> The ambiguity attached to participation has helped to foster its own
> cause. Because so many different hopes have been linked with it, so
> many different expectations about what it will achieve, it has been
> embraced by spokesmen of highly varying political hues. Consumers
> have advocated participation in order to achieve their particular ends
> and the service providers have similarly welcomed it in order to serve
> theirs. The very uncertainty of its impact has enabled a common rally-
> ing call.
>
> (Richardson 1983: 99)

This chapter will explore the many meanings associated with the concepts
of public involvement or participation in state services. The dictionary
definition of 'involvement' is '. . . to include, to be part of', while that for
'participation' is '. . . to take part in', implying a less passive and more
specific activity than involvement. This difference will be explored further
in this chapter but, for simplicity of presentation, 'involvement' will be used
as the generic term. A distinction will also be made throughout between
the forms of public involvement, the values associated with them and the
context in which they take place. While the term 'involvement' is typically
used to refer to a process which leads to a set of 'good things', such as
influence and empowerment, accountability and open government, human
interaction and social responsibility, it is also the case that some forms of
involvement may, in certain contexts, act as barriers to or diversions from
the desired outcomes.

One reason for the ambiguity of the concept of public involvement is
that it can be seen as both as means to an end and an end in itself.

Bacharach (1975: 40), for example, argues that, by enabling individuals to make decisions that affect them and their communities, involvement '. . . is an essential means for an individual to discover his real needs through the intervening discovery of himself as a social human being'. Seeing involvement as a basic human need, however, may serve to obscure its connection with wider social and political agendas. It is important that the context of involvement, and particularly the power relations by which it is constituted, is appreciated in order fully to assess its value and consequences. This chapter will begin by describing two very different approaches to public involvement: the consumerist and the democratic. These approaches will be used to explore the connections between the 'means' of involvement and the 'ends' it is designed to serve. The chapter will then examine the different forms and processes of involvement and will conclude with a discussion of the history of public involvement in state services in the UK in the post-war years.

## Democratic and consumerist approaches

Two broad approaches to public involvement can be identified in the literature: the democratic and the consumerist. The democratic approach relates to people primarily in their capacities as citizens and taxpayers with rights to use public services and duties to contribute or participate with others collectively in the society in which they live. This approach emphasizes the importance of equity and empowerment with 'participation' being seen as a key concept. Public services have traditionally been viewed as a demonstration of the state's commitment to provide its citizens with the means to participate equally in all aspects of social and political life. Underpinning the democratic approach therefore are two principles: first, that public participation should be encouraged because it is beneficial to maintaining a healthy democracy and assists people to fulfil the obligations of citizenship; and second that the full diversity of interests and allegiances in society should be represented in the political process.

As we have seen, the consumerist approach, in contrast, is based on the market relationships of the private sector. It emphasizes the importance of the organization identifying the preferences of individual consumers to enhance its market competitiveness. The decision about the most appropriate mechanisms for consumer involvement is thus a management responsibility. The emphasis of this approach is on the rights of consumers to information, access, choice and redress in relation to a specific service or product. The issues of whether an individual qualifies for, or has the resources to use, the service in the first place are not addressed.

The two approaches have different implications for the extent and nature of public involvement. Whereas the consumerist model views involvement as a series of discrete episodes, the democratic model may encompass a more developmental and incremental process in which those participating broaden their perspectives and experiences through collective action. Again, while the role of the public in the consumerist model is defined in a limited way in relation to a specific act of consumption or service use, the democratic model, in theory at least, enables the citizen to bring multiple roles and experiences to the participation process.

## Influence, power and empowerment

### Influence

One of the primary justifications for popular democratic involvement is that it enables people to influence the decisions that affect their lives. It is important, however, to acknowledge the possibility of involvement without influence as well as of influence without involvement. Hirschman's (1970) concepts of 'exit', 'voice' and 'loyalty' provide a broad framework for understanding the options available to consumers to exercise influence in a market system. Consumers can stop using a service (exit) and go elsewhere, providing there are accessible alternatives, or they can try to influence the service by expressing an opinion (voice) using complaint systems, consultation opportunities, etc. Even if not completely satisfied with a service, however, consumers may continue to use it without voicing their dissatisfaction, because of factors such as convenience, vulnerability or commitment to the product (loyalty).

In a fairly passive sense of the word, exit and loyalty could be viewed as types of involvement in the market, but it may be more appropriate to view them as forms of influence without involvement. Hirschman's model distinguishes the one-way relationship of exit and loyalty from the more interactive process of voice. However, these activities are not unrelated: the degree of actual influence exerted by voice, for example, will be related to the opportunities for choice (exit) and the factors which hold people to a particular service (loyalty). A consumer who is dependent on limited access to an essential service may be unwilling to use voice to express dissatisfaction if opportunities to go elsewhere are not easily available. Equally a service or organization may be more likely to listen to the voice of its customers when there is a realistic possibility of losing them to competitors. The expression of voice however may also be limited by feelings of loyalty to the service/product or effectively silenced by organizations preferring to encourage exit rather than deal with troublesome customers.

The idea of interaction or voice is elaborated further in a model developed by Arnstein (1969). Working within the democratic approach, Arnstein prefers the term 'participation' to that of 'involvement' precisely because of its emphasis on interaction. Unlike Hirschman, moreover, who sees voice or interaction as necessarily a good thing, she is aware of the extent to which public participation is subject to the operation of wider power relations which may serve to frustrate or distort the desired outcomes. Arnstein identifies a range of different types or levels of participation and

8 Citizen control ⎫
7 Delegated power ⎬ Degrees of citizen power
6 Partnership ⎭
5 Placation ⎫
4 Consultation ⎬ Degrees of tokenism
3 Informing ⎭
2 Therapy ⎫
1 Manipulation ⎬ Non-participation

**Figure 4.1** Arnstein's ladder of citizen participation.
*Source*: Arnstein 1969

then presents them in the form of a 'ladder' in relation to who holds the power and the extent of influence involved. On the first rungs of the ladder are participation exercises designed to ensure a 'feel-good' factor, giving people a voice as a way of making them feel involved, improving their skills in working together or ensuring their compliance. This level of participation involves little commitment to, or possibilities for, real influence. Examples given include groups run in residential establishments, consumer surveys undertaken as public relation exercises or statutory consultation exercises where real decisions have already been taken.

The next rung of the ladder is about information giving, with the power to define what the information will be remaining in the hands of the instigators of the exercise. 'Consultation', which seeks to listen to the views of participants before decisions are made, is a further move up the ladder particularly if accompanied by a commitment to act on the views expressed. 'Placation' is the next step, offering a very limited role for public participation within a much wider area of decision making. This could involve choosing the colour of the curtains in residential accommodation, for example, or the layout of an adventure playground. The higher rungs of the ladder identify forms of participatory activity in which the public has greater power, where there is a commitment to ongoing activity and where a developmental approach exists to integrate the views of the participants fully within the wider decision-making process. 'Citizen control', illustrated by examples of user-led projects, community initiatives and locally run services, is accorded the highest rung on the ladder (Figure 4.1).

By linking Arnstein's idea of a ladder of participation with Hirschman's concepts of voice and exit, Hoggett (1992) identifies a number of different ways in which the service user can exert influence at both individual and collective levels. In a managed market, where the user is rarely the direct purchaser of a service, she can nevertheless be involved in decisions about whether and what kind of services are provided, via the production of a care plan, for example, or by participating in some kind of service feedback. She may also be able to increase her influence over more strategic decisions, such as the patterns of service delivery or the identification of need, by joining with other users of the service to form a service-user group.

Hoggett's scenarios, however, depend on the individual being eligible for the role of service user. The option of 'voice' is only potentially empowering for those entitled to receive the service in question. As we have argued, wider questions about the 'politics of eligibility' in the context of public services are not addressed in the consumerist approach. Consideration of these and other factors influencing the wider political context of public involvement require consideration of the issue of power.

### Power

It is possible to examine the significance of power to the process of public involvement using the three-dimensional analysis developed by Lukes (1974). In the first (one-dimensional) or pluralist explanation of power each side is seen to know its own interests which it struggles to assert in a visible and open decision-making process. The battle may be unequal in that some groups wield more power than others but the diversity of the political process ensures that no single group will dominate overall. In the 'two-dimensional' understanding of power, however, the relationship between the sides is viewed as more complex: those without power may know their interests, but their ability to secure them may be constrained by the ability of the powerful to control the political agenda. The exercise of power, moreover, may involve inaction as well as covert or overt action on the part of those with strong vested interests. The successful monopoly by professionals over the definition of the issues in public services can be viewed as an example of the 'two-dimensional' explanation of power. In a 'three-dimensional' analysis, power is seen to be exercised through the operation of cultural processes and social structures as well as by the actions of individuals or groups; such invisible influences may not only limit the ability of those without power to articulate and pursue their interests, but may crucially undermine their ability to recognise these interests in the first place. Servian (1996), for example, suggests the relevance of the theory of 'learned helplessness' (Seligman 1972), in which individuals are rewarded for behaving passively, to a three-dimensional understanding of power.

Linking the different explanations of power identified by Lukes to Arnstein's model of participation suggests that forms of public participation may be established which appear to give people influence when viewed in terms of a single-dimensional explanation of power, but which are actually used to prevent certain issues from being discussed. By channelling interaction to a limited agenda, attention can be diverted from areas of potential conflict that those with power wish to avoid. Seen in this way, participatory mechanisms can serve as a means of social control by preventing challenges to the status quo. By engaging people and giving them responsibility in a particular area of policy or service, moreover, the process of public participation may also serve to contain criticism and unrest by helping the public to appreciate the realities of government and/or by implying public support for the decisions taken:

Participation can force, or educate, the participants to gain an awareness of governmental problems and policies and this will not only inhibit the public from pressing for solutions to their own problems, but will also enable the authorities to legitimise their decisions with the stamp of public approval.

(Dearlove 1973: 37)

Others argue, however, that even if limited in scope, or ambiguous in terms of its intentions, public participation may in some cases nevertheless serve as an effective means of reconciling or constituting diverse and potentially competing interests. Thus Richardson stresses the positive aspects of the process of participation:

The process of discussion and negotiation between participants facilitates the decisions likely to prove more acceptable to all sides . . . the bargaining process can be seen as a socially desirable means of reaching the accommodation of seemingly incompatible interests . . . it is exactly through the pressures and counter-pressures of political debate that a real understanding of the interests involved can be achieved.

(Richardson 1983: 126)

Whilst acknowledging that too often the rhetoric of participation can lead to false assumptions about the actual balance of power involved, Richardson argues that, nevertheless, in some cases it can serve to politicize those involved and encourage additional forms of political involvement. One potential outcome of the process of discussion and negotiation may thus be the political 'empowerment' of those involved.

## Empowerment

Appreciation of the concept of empowerment is fundamental to an understanding of involvement and participation. As with the latter two concepts, 'empowerment' is used to refer to a number of very different situations and similarly suffers from a lack of clarity and definition. Servian (1996), for example, identifies nine different uses of the term ranging from access to the democratic process and spiritual enlightenment, through freedom from government and advocacy, to the impact of changes introduced by new technology. Centrally he highlights the use of empowerment to describe a process in which individuals are enabled to meet their own needs. Quoting the definition of needs given by Doyal and Gough (1991), in which the first principles of human life are seen to be autonomy and survival, he identifies a further definition of empowerment as 'moves towards autonomy' (Servian 1996: 9).

There are different philosophies of empowerment contained within the democratic and consumerist approaches. The democratic approach sees the empowerment of the citizen occurring via wider socio-political processes such as the redistribution of income, the creation of the welfare state and the development of social rights. Whilst the democratic approach also encompasses a range of more specific and localized developments such as decentralized services, mechanisms for direct participation and funding for community development and voluntary activity, it has been criticized for its focus on macro-level changes rather than on the micro-level of individuals' daily experience of service use.

In contrast, the consumerist approach to empowerment focuses on individuals and their need for information, access, choice and redress in relation to specific services/products. Although the 'voice' option is given a high prominence in the requirements for audit and quality assurance, in reality the consumerist approach sees 'choice' and 'exit' as the primary mechanisms for individual empowerment. Implicit within this approach, however, is an ideal typical notion of a rational individual making self-interested decisions which may fail to take account of the differences in people's ability to behave as active consumers. Recent research by Baldcock and Ungerson (1994) on individuals experiencing strokes, for example, found that that while some people's behaviour came close to that of the 'ideal type' market consumer, many more assumed an essentially passive role in the face of this physical health crisis. The wide range of information offered to help people make choices appeared to have little actual impact on the majority of individuals. Particularly in the context of health services, as we have seen, the ability of individuals to act as market consumers may be undermined by the inequality of knowledge and information that exists between producer and consumer.

In assessing the contemporary relevance of Arnstein's ladder of participation, critics such as Hallett (1987) highlight its failure to consider the role of professional expertise within the participation process. Arnstein considered the input of professionals to be disempowering in all circumstances, but Hallett points out that the connection between participation and influence requires citizens to understand complex issues. This in turn requires them to tap into expertise, a process which can be enhanced by the facilitation of professionals. Williamson (1992) illustrates the importance of professionals acting as allies to consumer groups seeking change within the NHS.

The strength of Arnstein's approach lies in its emphasis on the nature of empowerment as a developmental process. Much public involvement appears to be planned in a one-off and ad hoc manner typically to respond to a particular requirement to demonstrate consumer input to a wider service audit. There may be little understanding of, or commitment to, any longer-term process (Taylor and Lupton 1995). The attempt by the Office of Public Management (1992) to develop levels of participation is a good example of this problem. In its promotion of an essentially 'horizontal' approach to public involvement, the document implies that it is for managers to decide at which level they wish to pitch their initiatives (see Table 4.1). Levels are treated as stand-alone packages to be used in whichever combination of 'mix and match' appears appropriate at the time. Such an approach, however, effectively ensures that public participation remains at

**Table 4.1** Office of Public Management – continuum of involvement

| Continuum of involvement ⟶ | | | | | | |
|---|---|---|---|---|---|---|
| Giving information to the public | Educating the public to equip it for participation | Learning from consumers/ the public about views of services | Learning from consumers/ the public about their needs | Consulting consumers/ the public about healthcare priorities | Planning individual care with the service user | Inviting consumers/ the public to contribute to decision-making |

*Source*: Office of Public Management (1992).

the lowest rungs of the ladder. Representatives of the user movement, however, have argued that participation must be seen as a process comprising different steps or stages in which individuals develop their ability and willingness to participate over time. These steps include accessibility, clear information, support and advocacy, clarity of purpose and a commitment to acting on the results. It is possible thus to interpret the rungs on the Arnstein ladder in an incremental way, seeing involvement in micro-level decisions, such as choosing the colour of the curtains, as empowering if it is planned as a first step in a longer process leading to fuller involvement.

## Involvement, representation and accountability

### Direct and indirect involvement

Richardson (1983) identifies two forms of democratic participation. Direct participation brings people into personal contact with decision makers and covers the varied mechanisms set up by government for consultation, such as statutory meetings and advisory panels. Indirect participation includes all other activities in which people consciously attempt to exert some influence on decision making and policy formulation, such as voting, membership of political parties, campaigning and pressure group activity. This distinction can be linked to ideas about different types of democracy. The concept of direct participation reflects the classical Greek model of democracy, developed further by Rousseau and J.S. Mill, in which citizens are given the opportunity to meet their governors face to face to debate and discuss relevant issues of government. Indirect participation, in contrast, refers to a process in which opportunities for debate between governors and the governed are mediated by some form of representation. This type of participation is integral to more modern forms of representative democracy.

Richardson's twofold definition thus needs to be supplemented by a third type of participation. Her idea of direct participation is associated with the perspective of the governors as they are directly confronted by their citizens. However, from the citizen's point of view, there may be no direct contact with governors, because their views may be represented by others. In order to clarify representation from the citizen's perspective, therefore, the term 'mediated' representation will be used. The use of 'direct participation' will be limited to situations where citizens are in face-to-face relationships with governors. We will use the term 'indirect participation' as Richardson does to indicate all other forms of citizen participation which attempt to achieve influence. Forms of social participation, such as volunteering or self-help activities, are particularly interesting insofar as they can be viewed either as a form of action in themselves or as a means of underpinning and stimulating either direct or indirect political participation.

Despite the rhetoric of consumerism, with its emphasis on individuals representing their own interests, the concept of mediated representation is particularly important for understanding the connections between involvement, influence and accountability. It is possible to identify four different forms of mediated representation: elected representation, professional representation or advocacy, provider representation within managed markets and statistical representation. Before examining these different types of representation, however, it is necessary to clarify what is meant by the term. Although typically related in everyday language to the operation of representative democracy, the use of the term, like many others we have considered, is subject to considerable imprecision (Squires 1994: 1): '. . . the concept of representation lies at the very heart of our claim to democratic status and yet it is little theorised and practically confused.'

Traditionally, the exercise of representative democracy involves choosing representatives for national and local government based on geographical constituencies and linked to the policies of a political party. It is also based on the premise of universal suffrage: equal participation by all citizens. The principles of this system are widely replicated, with some adaptations, in the mechanisms for indirect and social participation within civic, community and voluntary organizations. Once elected there is some expectation that representatives will keep in touch with their constituents and broadly follow the policies put forward at election, while retaining some autonomy to follow their individual consciences. Critics of this system, however, point to the decreasing relevance of geographical area or 'space' as a basis for representation as well as to the breakdown of allegiances deriving from class or employment status. In their place has grown a wide range of separate pressure groups based on identity (gay rights/women's groups/black communities), single issues or campaigns (environmental/ animal rights lobbies) or, in the context of health and welfare services, on individuals' current or potential use of a service (disability lobbies/tenant and claimant groups). These groups have attempted to raise the profile and further the interests of specific constituents dissatisfied with the limited representation of formal electoral systems. One of their main demands has been for service users to be enabled to speak on their own behalf rather than through representatives who may not understand or share their particular experiences (Lindow 1993). Significantly, however, these groups are organized on democratic principles and may themselves struggle with the issues of representation and the best means to achieve influence.

Professional representation and advocacy involves professionals representing the interests of their clients or patients on an individual or collective basis. The professionals argue that they are well placed to fulfil this role because of their close relationships with individuals who, due to their circumstances, may be less able to represent their own interests. Critics of this form of representation suggest that professionals may tend to emphasise the passivity of their clients in order to ensure full recognition of their own expertise. Nevertheless, the approach has become well established in the new health and social care market place via the role of the care manager in the personal social services, for example, or the GP as 'patient's proxy' in healthcare purchasing. Closely linked to the idea of professional representation is that of provider representation, where those providing services make their case for resources on the basis of information gained from consumerist methods of public involvement. This method is open to the same criticism levelled at the professional approach, namely the possibility of providers manipulating the results of consumer involvement to serve their own interests. While individual consumers have opportunities for more direct ways of representing their views, via complaints systems or legal action, they may not be easily able to use these methods.

Statistical representation involves the use of scientific methods to select a sample from a given population in order to carry out survey or market research. Here the term 'representation' refers to a given set of characteristics found in a particular population, typically attributes such as age, sex or employment status, but is open to a wide range of variables considered significant by those instigating the exercise. The statistical approach is favoured by consumerists because it is firmly linked to the ideal of individuals representing their own interests without engaging in complex forms of decision making that are not immediately relevant to their experience. It may derive from a general distrust of anyone attempting to represent the interests of others. Consultation through surveys and opinion polls may appear to enable access to a wider range of views and opinions than is possible through an elected representative system.

However, the apparent objectivity of these methods may serve to obscure important issues of equity and participation. People need to understand written questions, be willing and able to fill in questionnaires or take part in interviews. Crucially, this approach only addresses the motivation of respondents to participate at a very superficial level, through their need for information, access or reward. There is no overt recognition of the processes of support that people may require to take part or to become 'informed' citizens. Statistical representation will only address power differentials in the involvement process if the instigators choose to reflect them in the sampling techniques. Ironically, it may be precisely those with greatest access to other forms of indirect and social participation who are most likely to respond to these opportunities for involvement. Recognition that information gained in this form of market research is limited in scope, particularly in relation to the level of feedback required for public services, has led to the development of a range of more participatory methods emphasizing dialogue and interaction, such as focus groups, critical incident techniques, deliberative polling and Citizen Juries (Stewart *et al.* 1995). These approaches will be described in more detail in later chapters.

Barnes *et al.* (1995) identify a further type of representation, referred to as 'typical', which appears to combine aspects of both the statistical and the democratic approach. People are selected as being typical of the characteristics of a particular group or population, with advice on selection being provided by members of relevant interest groups. The sample selected is then asked to participate in some kind of substantive consultative or participatory exercise, often taking place over an extended time period. The user movement has been instrumental in promoting this approach as a realistic way of including a user perspective within the full decision-making process whilst avoiding the problem of a few individuals claiming to speak on behalf of the many. Significantly, however, those in the user movement argue that, if service users are to perform these roles effectively, such an approach requires an appropriate infrastructure underpinned by sufficient resources.

Generally, there seems to be less common ground between the consumerist and democratic approaches in relation to the issue of representation than in any other area so far discussed. In particular, the comparison indicates a central difference between the two types of representation in terms of their approach to the issue of responsibility or accountability. Whereas in the democratic model, accountability lies essentially with the individual representative, in the consumerist approach it rests with those who instigate the various forms of public consultation or involvement. In the democratic model, moreover, the notion of public representation is fundamental to effective political decision making whereas in the consumerist model it may play only a very small part in the wider process of performance management.

## Accountability

The issue of accountability is discussed in greater depth in Chapter 3. Here we are concerned to highlight the key differences in the type and forms of accountability involved in the democratic and consumerist approaches. As we have seen, accountability is central to the democratic model and is encapsulated in the idea of 'open government'. Boaden *et al.* (1982) identify three levels of open government. The first concentrates on the flow of information between the governed and those who govern, emphasizing the importance of government publicizing its intentions and developing ways of collecting information back from relevant populations. The second level focuses on the need for government to increase the transparency of the decision-making process by opening its meetings to the public and the press.

The third level of open government provides a more active role for the public by emphasizing the importance of governors developing mechanisms for more extensive interaction between themselves and those they govern.

These three levels involve different perceptions on the part of governors about the value of direct contact with their populations and the relevance of public input to the business of decision making. The validity of public involvement is also influenced by the power of other vested interests such as those of the professionals to define the issues for debate and the solutions to identified problems. The importance of public participation at any one point in time is also affected by how well the governors perceive that their decisions are being received, as evidenced by the popularity of participatory schemes before elections, after episodes of social unrest and/or where research indicates the failure of existing services to meet identified needs.

In the pure market model accountability is entirely aimed at shareholders who have both formal and effective control over managers via their right to 'exit', to sell their share in a poorly performing company and buy into others that promise greater 'shareholder value'. The main opportunity for 'voice' on the part of shareholders is via the annual general meeting – the 'parliament' of the market. The accountability of a company to its shareholders, however, is not matched by any formal lines of accountability to its consumers; a situation encapsulated by the phrase *caveat emptor* ('let the buyer beware'). In fact, in order to protect consumers, the pure market model is regulated by legal and political processes which provide certain rights in respect of the products purchased. These rights, moreover, have been secured by political and consumer groups working within the democratic process to gain legitimacy for their concerns.

As discussed in Chapter 3, the development of the public sector has been increasingly characterized by the dominance of private sector approaches to accountability. The separation of policy and administration and the erosion of local democratic involvement means that managers' main concern lies with the implementation of decisions taken at the central political level (increasingly on the basis of Cabinet, rather than parliamentary decision making). The requirements of upward accountability, moreover, are such that they leave little space for anything other than fairly tokenistic forms of accountability at a local level:

> [T]he present system, which usually involves rigorous and prescriptive upline accountability, has a loose 'do-it yourself' approach to ... accountability to the wider public, usually only specifying the publication of an annual report or annual open meeting. Governance, it is argued, is relatively unimportant if the organisation can be observed to be achieving its objectives.
>
> (Plummer 1994: 4)

In this context, it becomes easier for managers to discharge their limited responsibility for local accountability by means of instruments which can be carefully controlled and which do not encourage come-back or ongoing debate. The market survey, for example, is a highly visible way for those running public services to be seen to take the views of local citizens into account whilst remaining a limited, and therefore 'safe', instrument which does not impel action in the same way as do mechanisms such as performance review, inspection or audit. Interaction with the members of the public as a result becomes particularized and fragmented, focused on issues surrounding the delivery of specific services. Wider public decision making is discouraged and involvement de-politicized as accountability to the citizen-elector is replaced by accountability to the citizen-consumer.

## Involvement and participation in public services

Previous chapters have identified the key features characterizing the development of public services over the last two decades. In order fully to review the role of public involvement, however, it is necessary to take a rather longer historical perspective. Given that the formal recognition of the consumerist approach is relatively new, this historical overview will mainly focus on involvement in the democratic tradition and on collective action rather than involvement at the individual level.

Traditionally, citizen participation and involvement stemmed from two quite distinct traditions based on differences in social class. The middle and upper classes helped those less fortunate than themselves through volunteering and charitable works. Whilst this experience spawned social reformers who successfully campaigned to improve the social condition of the poor, much was also concerned with maintaining the status quo. In contrast, the participatory experience of the poor and working classes derived from the experience of privation and need. Working class self-help and labour movements were overtly committed to social change and emphasized equality, self-improvement and collective ways of working.

At its inception in the 1940s, the welfare state represented the replacement of the existing piecemeal provision of state, charitable and self-help services with a comprehensive system of state support covering individuals from the 'cradle to the grave'. As we have argued, public services were seen to reflect the state's commitment to provide the means for all its citizens to participate equally in social life. For the majority of the public and policy makers, the vision of the welfare state represented a new social contract between the state and its citizens, leaving behind the privations of the war time economy, the uncertainties of self-reliance and the paternalism of charitable approaches. Traditions of self-help and voluntary work still remained, but without a clearly identified role in the new welfare system. Their importance was acknowledged however in Beveridge's lesser known report on *Voluntary Action* (Beveridge 1948) which maintained that voluntarism should continue to provide 'a human face' to complement the state's role in allocating resources. He also saw it as one way in which people could continue to perform their duties as citizens as well as achieve their rights. The term 'voluntarism' is used by Beveridge not just to refer to charitable volunteering, but to a wide range of participatory activities in which people contributed to their communities. Gladstone (1979), in his review of the voluntary sector thirty years later, reveals that at the end of his life Beveridge felt that the subsequent development of public services had not fully reflected this vision. As Richard Crossman (1976) made clear in his diaries at the time, few other politicians shared this concern, believing rather that the need for voluntary action would lessen as the welfare state developed.

By the 1960s, this Utopian ideal was beginning to fade with the growing realization that state provision was not achieving the aims set for it. In part this was due to the slow and limited development of Beveridge's vision (Leonard and Corrigan 1978) with many welfare services still provided in the traditional charitable mould by the voluntary sector. In addition, as early as the 1950s, the limitations of state provision began to spawn new types of participation in more overtly campaigning activities, such as the 'squatting' movement (Bailey and Brake 1975):

> The alternative organisations, groups and movements that grew up in the 1960s and 70s were in many ways the by-product of the public welfare system; as much a reaction of frustration to the deficiencies, size and inaccessibility of the state welfare apparatus as the result of pressures to participate and protest engendered by the wider process of social and cultural change.
>
> (Brenton 1985: 36)

Significantly, much of this new type of voluntary action was organized around the consumption or use of particular services, focusing either on gaps in state provision or the inappropriate nature of current services. Its major aim was to lobby the Government to provide for particular social groups not adequately served by existing services. Thus while their focus was often on consumer issues, the mode of operation of these new forms of voluntary action was firmly based in the popular democratic approach. At times this development entailed voluntary groups undertaking experimental projects in order to demonstrate new ways of working. In turn, this led to several being funded by government to provide specialist or innovative services directly. Some established voluntary organizations with their roots in nineteenth century paternalism took this opportunity to rethink their roles and forge alliances with this new movement, harnessing their resources and management expertise to the new energy for reform and change.

These changes formed the basis for the development of the 'new voluntarism' of the 1960s and 1970s which combined the role of innovative and complementary service provision with that of campaigning for change. This combination of approaches led to some tensions within the activities and management structures of the organizations involved. One was the dilemma, experienced by organizations like the pre-school movement, of providing an experimental service to address the particular needs of a group or community whilst continuing to lobby for greater state provision. Another tension in some of the new hybrid organizations emerged between the collective and participatory approaches of the labour movement and the paternalistic ethos of traditional voluntarism.

The 1960s saw many politicians rediscovering the possibilities of 'voluntary action' with David Owen (1965: 20) as Minister for Health maintaining that the new Labour Government did not want to establish a state monopoly of welfare but wished rather to adhere to the 'principle of partnership' between statutory and voluntary activity. The end of the 1960s thus saw the first examples of governments sponsoring participation as a conscious policy decision, something which the state would be responsible for stimulating and funding rather than just responding to. In part, this shift was a political reaction, not only to expressions of growing public dissatisfaction with public services, but also to concerns about social unrest within inner cities, low turn-outs at general and local elections and research indicating that the desired outcomes of public services were not being achieved (Seebohm Report 1968; Plowden Report 1969).

In particular, there was a growing concern that public services were creating an increasingly demanding, but essentially passive citizenry. A number of government reports on different public services were published promoting the idea of community participation and involvement. The Skeffington Report (1969) advocating public participation in local planning and housing redevelopment was quickly followed by the Plowden Report (1969) favouring parent and community support for schools. The Seebohm Report (1968) on social services, making the case for larger and more integrated social services departments, similarly stressed the need for community development to be undertaken alongside mainstream casework.

This new interest in public participation must be seen as part of a wider concern about the efficiency of public services which was emerging in these years, particularly about the way these services were managed and organised. The beginning of the 1970s saw large-scale reorganization of public services into bigger, more integrated, departments with a stronger emphasis on corporate management. This was interpreted by some commentators (Bennington 1978) as undermining the ability of local elected representatives to play an effective part in the management of public services. It is of some significance that this reorganization coincided with funding for community development and voluntary activity through initiatives such as Urban Aid and the Community Development projects of 1970–4.

It is also relevant to note that the new interest in participation began to involve local authority managers directly, whilst previously the main focus for contact with the public and community groups had been local authority councillors and the local democratic process. Whilst some members saw this new interest on the part of their officers as helpful and complementary to their role, there were inevitably some areas of conflict. This was most likely to occur when officers identified opinions and interests on the part of the public which were contrary to those held by its political representatives.

This situation caused problems for some local authority staff employed as community development workers when their activities displeased their employers. As a result, the 1970s witnessed many examples of short-lived community development initiatives as well as considerable debate about where such activity should best be located.

In this period, the commitment to public participation was apparent in public funding for initiatives involving both direct and indirect participation. Community development initiatives and finance for the voluntary sector was made available to stimulate indirect forms of participation and involvement. Public funding and grants from large charities such as the Gulbenkian Foundation were given in recognition of the continuing inequalities between geographical areas, especially between the inner and outer cities, and between particular groups in the population. At the same time, and partly as a response to the demands of community organizations and pressure groups, some public services such as local authority housing departments were beginning to set up mechanisms for direct participation, such as tenant advisory groups and neighbourhood forums.

As Boaden *et al.* (1982) point out, there has been a constant tension in the management of public services between the objectives of efficiency and those of democracy. The case for efficiency favours larger service delivery units to achieve economies of scale whilst the case for democratic accountability leans towards smaller scale operations in which to involve the public more actively. This tension has been expressed in the continuous disagreement between local and central government about where the balance of public sector decision making should lie and was particularly apparent in the NHS reorganizations of 1974 and 1982 (see Chapter 5). Whilst the overriding trend has been towards greater central control in all services, the requirement, albeit often symbolic, to address issues of local community involvement and representation remains.

The growing impact of professionalism during the late 1960s and 1970s provides another important dimension to the debates about public involvement. The rationale of professionalism is to seek control over both the definition of the problem and the means by which it is solved or alleviated, as well as over decisions about who is eligible to receive the service (Johnson 1972). This is done by claims to specialist knowledge and expertise as well as by the use of language and concepts comprehensible only to other members of the profession concerned. The rise of new professional groupings throughout the public sector, in both the delivery and administration of services, had a significant impact on lay involvement. In the face of claims to professional expertise and authority, the credibility of elected representatives and lay managers became more difficult to sustain and the role of service users became increasingly passive. Williamson's discussion of the experience of consumer influence in the NHS reveals the often overt resistance of the professional culture to lay participation and to conceding credibility to any perspectives other than its own (Williamson 1992). However, against this, it must be noted that the professional response to participation has not been entirely one of resistance; some professional groups have welcomed the opportunity to work with the public as a way of gaining or confirming support for their concerns in the face of the scepticism of elected representatives or managers.

By the late 1970s, as we have seen, the continued poor performance of the UK economy was fuelling concerns about the escalating cost of welfare spending. The election of a Conservative Government in 1979 heralded radical changes in thinking about the place and role of welfare (see Chapter 2). As the new prime minister, Margaret Thatcher, announced, this new thinking included a revitalized role for voluntary or 'volunteer' activity: 'The volunteer movement is at the heart of all our social welfare provision . . . it can do things which government cannot do, or it can do them better' (speech to the WRVS, 1980, quoted in Ungerson 1985: 213). This change of emphasis had a slow but profound impact on the experiences of those involved in direct and indirect participation. Firstly, some commentators (Gladstone 1979; Hadley and Hatch 1981) began to interpret the new manifestation of 'voluntarism' and community organization as evidence of the potential for a new 'welfare pluralism' in which the monopoly of statutory organizations was broken and a range of voluntary organizations and local community groups could take a greater part in the provision of public services. This approach was particularly developed in ideas about the localization of services into smaller areas or 'patches' and given backing in the report by the Barclay Committee (1982) on community social work in which professionals were urged to work more closely with their local communities in the provision of social care.

Secondly, a number of local councils sought to address the criticisms of public services by a process of decentralization which established neighbourhood offices. Local officers from different services were encouraged to work more closely together and with local groups to develop more effective and responsive services tailored to the needs of their particular communities. The Housing Act 1980 gave added impetus to this by enshrining tenant participation in its legislation. The subsequent changes in public services towards privatization and marketization during the 1980s and 1990s further extended these developments in public involvement and participation. Moves were made to increase the role of the public, for example, in housing and education: the Education Reform Act 1988 enabled parents, by a simple majority vote, to 'opt out' of the local education system and directly manage their own schools; the Housing Acts of 1980 and 1986 provided tenants both with the individual right to buy their houses and the opportunity collectively to transfer the ownership of their estate to a different landlord. As discussed in earlier chapters, consumerism in this way became part of the accepted discourse of public services.

Finally, the role identified for the voluntary sector in the privatization of public service functions has a fundamental impact on its funding and development. The new arrangements for the internal market introduced by the NHS and Community Care Act 1990 were designed to encourage voluntary and not-for-profit organizations to compete with private and statutory providers in the provision of mainstream services. In a climate of reduced funding the emphasis has increasingly been placed on funding for specific services with tight adherence to contract specifications. This has had a major impact on middle level voluntary organizations. Most importantly, there has been a separation of service provision from other types of activity such as campaigning, research and development. As we have seen, in the past new and innovative services often grew out of a combination of these activities, with activists becoming involved in defining more appropriate services. The emphasis within the 'contract culture', however, on specific and tangible outcomes may serve to discourage the more developmental and open-ended type of activity associated with some voluntary groups. Increasingly, distinctions are being made between the core service function, which is funded, and other functions, which are defined as peripheral and not appropriate for public funding.

While the earlier growth in the size of public service organizations was seen to reduce local accountability and involvement, the opposite trend towards the decentralization and 'downsizing' of services is promoted as ensuring greater responsiveness and choice to the service user. However, while this may be true to an extent, it may also be the case that, by imposing a narrow service function on many voluntary and community organizations, the aim of increased local responsiveness is frustrated in the longer term. Those organizations which have traditionally played a key role in stimulating and supporting the indirect forms of involvement and participation which underpin formal involvement processes may no longer have the capacity or flexibility to carry out this role. Moreover, in their focus on individual choice, such developments may also serve to diminish the potential contribution of more participatory and collective forms of activity to ensuring that services are responsive to the needs of wider communities and the public as a whole. Chapter 5 examines the extent to which and ways in which these tendencies have been played out in the specific context of the NHS.

# 5 The history of public involvement in health

## Introduction

The previous chapters have explored the key themes of citizenship, public management, accountability and the consumerist and democratic approaches to public involvement. In Chapter 4, the historical context of public participation in the public sector was charted. This chapter examines the development of public involvement in the UK national health service. As Klein (1995) has argued, the history of the NHS is one of a continued tension between local and central lines of accountability. Established as a centralized bureaucracy in 1948, the health service has always operated within a localized structure with regional and hospital boards, area health authorities and, most recently, district health authorities acting with management capacity and responsible to centrally appointed, local committees. Following the initial compromise made by Bevan over the structure and organization of the service – and in particular the concessions made to the medical profession (Honigsbaum 1989) – the NHS evolved into a powerful, medically dominated organization, where doctors made key decisions about the care of their patients and, consequently, about the allocation of resources at a local level.

Over the last half century, successive governments have wrestled with the inherent tensions enshrined in the birth of the NHS. Changes to the service have attempted variously to strengthen medical control of the NHS, challenge the tenets of centralized accountability, confront centralized and professional power and, most recently, undermine the dominance of the medical profession (Harrison and Pollitt 1994). As importantly, the last 25 years have been marked by growing public involvement in the NHS beyond that afforded by the role of the patient. This chapter describes the development of public and lay involvement in healthcare from the pre-NHS situation to the NHS and Community Care Act 1990 and traces the roots of current debates about consumerism, citizenship and the continued preoccupation with accountability.

Although essentially descriptive, the chapter identifies four key dichotomies or tensions inherent in the development of the NHS which, it argues, continue to shape much of the current debate about public involvement. These are: central and local accountability; professional and managerial power; professional and lay control; and individual and collective approaches. These dichotomies are not easily separable from each other, being entwined in complex relationships. Thus, the issue of professionalism and lay power is caught within the tensions between managerial and professional power, and these tensions in turn are played out in the context of shifts between central and local accountability. In order fully to comprehend these tensions or dichotomies, they must be placed within the historical development of the NHS. The chapter thus charts their progress through the pre-NHS period, the early years of consolidation up to the 1960s, the surfacing of tensions in the 1970s and 1980s and the developments leading up to the NHS reforms in 1991. It concludes by demonstrating the way in which these tensions continue to underpin the development of a consumerist approach in the post-internal market NHS.

## Establishing the NHS: the introduction of citizen rights?

The establishment of the NHS in 1948 changed the relationship between the public and the health service from one which was essentially market and charity based, to one that was underpinned by the notion of citizen rights. While the situation prior to the Second World War involved some elements of statutory insurance (introduced in 1911) covering general practice services for working men, access to healthcare for the majority of the population was based on the ability to pay and/or restricted to the hospital services provided by charities and local authorities. The voluntary hospitals relied substantially on paying patients and experienced difficulties in the pre-war period due to the low level of charitable funds and their inability to attract sufficient income from patients (Leathard 1990). The relationship between the public and healthcare services was an individualistic one, mirroring that of the doctor–patient and characterized by a commercial or insurance-based approach. The only collective arrangements for the nation's health were those provided by the local authorities, in particular the community health and public health (environmental health) services.

An element of democratic control over healthcare was afforded through the municipal health services, in particular the public health services and hospitals, and via the system of hospital boards. The opportunities for public involvement so provided, however, in terms of wielding municipal elected power or the administration of hospitals, were effectively restricted to the local 'great and the good'. Despite the fact that the early twentieth century was characterized by growing enfranchisement and changing political structures, the provision of most welfare services continued to reflect the traditional culture of charity and the inherent class and professional élitism of the wider society. There were significant exceptions to this rule, and the role of the Socialist Medical Association in developing the London County Council municipal medical scheme (Honigsbaum 1989) and important movements such as the Peckham Health Centre (Kenner 1986) should not be discounted.

The establishment of the NHS replaced this limited, but autonomous, involvement of local élites with a centralized structure. An accepted view is that its introduction represented a shift from an essentially individualized relationship between people and healthcare services to one based on universality and collectivist principles (Allsop 1995). However, such a simplistic understanding ignores the complexities of the arrangements and issues which surrounded the foundation of the service in 1948. Essentially, the establishment of the NHS was a compromise between the tensions of local and central politics, the power of the medical profession and the requirements of bureaucratic rationality (Klein 1995). In this context, Klein (1995: 70) suggests, members of the public were merely '. . . the ghosts in the NHS machinery'. The lay members of the regional health boards and local hospital management committees operated more as the agents of the Minister for Health than as local representatives and wider public involvement was limited to participation through the ballot box. Essentially, the relationship of the public to healthcare services remained encapsulated in the singleton role of the patient.

The 'contract' agreed with the medical profession in 1948 ensured the pivotal role of doctors in the management of the NHS through their membership of health boards and their ability to define appropriate healthcare. This degree of control was denied to other health professionals and to health administrators alike. In this way the institutional development of the NHS served to underpin the unequal power relationship between medical professionals and the public. This inequality was exacerbated by the fact that, with the establishment of the NHS, people were only given the right of *access* to healthcare services rather than the right to healthcare itself. This was an important distinction insofar as it effectively left decisions about who receives healthcare to the medical profession, as indicated in the following extract from a 1970 DHSS Memorandum:

> The health and personal social services have always operated on the basis that doctors and other professional providers of services have individual professional freedom to do what they consider to be right for their patients. Thus in each individual doctor–patient situation it is the doctor who decides on the appropriate objective and the appropriate priority.
>
> (Quoted in DHSS 1979)

Bevan's key reason for the development of a centralized service was to ensure the universality and equity of the service provided. This was undermined by the fact that, as a result of medical dominance, patients had no absolute right to particular medical treatments. Any such right was mediated by the medical practitioner, essentially the doctor, who had complete clinical freedom. So, rather than broadening citizen rights of access to all the population, the establishment of the NHS actually served to control and restrict access to healthcare resources. As the Memorandum continued: '. . . it is important to note that the existence of clinical freedom substantially reduces the ability of central authorities to determine objectives and priorities and to control individual facets of expenditure'. This situation remains unchanged today and has important implications for the development of public involvement to which we shall return at a later point. Bevan's vision of a universal service was further eroded by the continuation of geographical inequalities of provision across the country. The financial constraints surrounding the establishment of the NHS had served to reinforce, rather than remove these inequalities, with more affluent areas maintaining higher levels of provision.

One important concession made to the medical profession in return for its support of the NHS was that the service would not be run by the local authorities (Honigsbaum 1989). As a result, the health service was effectively split between the medical services (general practice and hospitals) which formed the core of the NHS, and the community or public health services (the medical officer of health, community nursing and environmental health) which remained under the control of the elected local authorities (Ottewill and Wall 1990). The principal argument for keeping public health services within local authorities was the connection with other local services such as housing, social services and planning. The concern was also about improving community, not just individual, health, the converse of the NHS with its focus on the individual patient. This dichotomy of provision continued as an undercurrent in the expanding healthcare system and provided the developing NHS with inherent managerial and accountability problems (Longley 1993) relating to the role of professionals and the balance between local autonomy and central control.

## The first thirty years: the consolidation of professional power and the birth of patient groups

The final shape of the NHS was thus the result of a series of political compromises and the inherent tensions between medical power, managerial accountability and public participation remained a constant theme in the successive reviews of the service from the 1950s onwards. In particular, the issue of central government or local authority control arose in a number of reports on the NHS including the Guillebaud Report (Guillebaud 1956), the 1968 Green Paper on NHS reorganization (DHSS 1968) and the Royal Commission on the NHS (DHSS 1979). The first and last of these rejected the idea of local authority control, while the Green Paper did not rule out the possibility of integrated health services under the control of the new type of local authorities then yet to be recommended by the Royal Commission on Local Government (Redcliffe-Maud 1969). The discussions in these documents did not question the role of the medical profession, although Guillebaud, in supporting the necessity of medical representation on regional health boards (RHBs) and hospital management committees (HMCs), did suggest that it should be limited to 25 per cent as, in some areas, the Committee had found representation of up to 42 per cent on RHBs and between 22 and 27 per cent on HMCs.

The medical profession, however, remained central to the operation of the NHS. Research has shown the degree to which doctors were able to reverse, veto, or heavily modify the decisions made by administrators, health authorities and the Ministry of Health (Harrison *et al.* 1990). The extent of the control that clinicians continued to wield over the shape of the service is effectively illustrated by the following quote from the 1962 Hospital Plan:

> ... the detailed recommendations of the Plan – the basic version of what a hospital service should be like – were almost entirely determined by medical consensus. There is no indication in the Hospital Plan of other possible criteria being considered, such as accessibility for patients or the effects of hospital size on staff morale or recruitment. The domination of the professional definition of the problem being tackled was all the greater for being implicit and unargued.
>
> (Klein 1995: 67)

Doctors themselves were accountable to the General Medical Council for extreme cases of clinical incompetence but, on the whole, the view of the profession was that doctors should be allowed to practise in whatever way they saw fit (Harrison and Pollitt 1994). The extent of non-extreme malpractice has not been researched but the fact that malpractice occurred and was inadequately dealt with, if at all, is now widely recognized (Rosenthal 1995). Given the emphasis placed on clinical freedom, the managerial accountability of doctors within the NHS was virtually non-existent. The idea of public accountability was similarly underdeveloped. In essence, the public, as individual patients, was assumed to be grateful for whatever was provided. In terms of more collective forms of participation, medical dominance combined with increased state provision to limit the role of voluntary agencies and charities in defining health issues and effectively to deny them any say in the running of the NHS. In part, this state of affairs reflected the general underdevelopment of voluntary activities in the health and welfare field in the immediate post-war period. By the 1960s, however, this situation was beginning to change.

*The first cracks: challenging the professionals*

The development of community and voluntary organizations within the healthcare field reflects the broader developments in public participation described in Chapter 4. Public involvement in healthcare, however, is characterized by a particular fragmentation resulting from the fact that patient or community groups have mainly developed around specific illnesses and diseases. There were two main exceptions to this rule: the first was the Patients' Association, established in 1963 to represent the patient interest as a whole; and the second was the growing interest in health issues taken by the more generic Consumer's Association. The Patients' Association originated from concerns over unsatisfactory individual treatment and, in particular, about research being undertaken on patients without their knowledge and consent. Its focus was, and has remained, primarily on the role of the public as individual patients: 'There is little of the radical flavour which sees the public services like health as a legitimate area for popular control' (Boaden *et al.* 1982: 127). Interestingly, the Patient's Association from the start represented an alliance between the public and the medical profession – which has always had members on the board – acting as patient advocates and lay representatives. As with health-related voluntary groups, alliances between the voluntary sector and the medical profession have typically been around specific service issues such as the campaign in the 1950s by local health authorities, the BMA and voluntary organizations working with elderly people for a publicly funded chiropody service (Ottewill and Wall 1990).

The first specific patient groups developed at the beginning of the 1960s with the establishment of organizations such as the Association for Improvements in Maternity Services (AIMS) in 1960 and the National Association for the Welfare of Children in Hospital (NAWCH) in 1961. Some suggest that their roots stretch back much further. Thus, Campbell (1990) has argued that the rise of mental health self-advocacy has common ground, with not only the Mental Patient's Union in the 1960s and 1970s, but also with the Alleged Lunatics' Friends Society of the 1860s and protesters in the 1940s and 1950s. The major development of voluntary organizations occurred, however, in the early 1970s. The origins of this growth have been explored in Chapter 4 although, in the specific context of the NHS, it is important to recognize the influence of changes in healthcare needs and provision. Increasingly, the population's need for healthcare was shifting towards support for people with long-term chronic illness and disability, thus exposing the social dimension of healthcare. As a result, the role of voluntary agencies changed from one of providing low-level, complementary support to one of campaigning for a better level of care for such groups and for a greater awareness of the social cost of illness. The national charity Age Concern, for example, had initially been established in the early 1940s as Old People's Welfare Committees to provide support to individual elderly people. Gradually it developed a proactive approach to the welfare of older people more generally through the establishment of a network of local committees and national offices. As a result of these developments, by the late 1960s there was a growing awareness of the role of voluntary organizations and interest groups in healthcare services.

The debate about the role of local authorities and local councillors had also raised concerns about the structure, management and accountability of the NHS (DHSS 1968; Redcliffe-Maud 1969). Although enacted by a Conservative government via the National Health Service Reorganisation Act 1973, the NHS reforms essentially adapted those developed by the Labour Government in the late 1960s. While the latter had called for more public involvement at a local level, however, Keith Joseph, the then Secretary of State for Health and Social Services, was concerned to change both the extent and nature of lay involvement. In an attempt to produce more viable and efficient boards, direct appointments prioritized people with business experience and local authority representation was reduced to 25 per cent. The approach taken was to separate lay involvement in health boards, designed to improve the management of the service, from the representation of the public interest, which would be provided by the establishment of the semi-independent Community Health Councils (CHCs – see later in this chapter). Despite this objective, few people with business skills were actually appointed to the boards and many within the Ministry and the NHS felt that it was inappropriate to attempt to do so, given that appointees typically lacked knowledge of the NHS and healthcare services (Klein 1995). Once again, we can see that the reorganization of the NHS was essentially the result of compromise between the medical profession's concern to retain power, the desire of local authorities to gain control and the determination of the centre to encourage more rational forms of managerial accountability.

At the same time as these developments were taking place, public and community health services were being removed from local authority control and brought within the NHS (Ottewill and Wall 1990) with a view to unifying healthcare provision under a single organization. While the discussions about local government reform had considered the option of placing healthcare services completely within the local authorities (Redcliffe-Maud 1969), this was not adopted due to concerns about the fragmented structure of local government. In essence, the arguments from the 1940s about the importance of the universality and comprehensiveness of the service were replayed and accepted yet again. The new structure which resulted, however, was complex, involving a number of layers of management from the Ministry through the regions, area health authorities and districts, with separate family practitioner committees (FPCs) to oversee family doctors and other independent practitioners (such as community pharmacists and dentists). The management structure was also hampered by the lack of clear lines of leadership and accountability, with multi-disciplinary groups managing by consensus (Edwards 1995).

The move of community and public health services from local councils to health authorities had an important impact on their operation. In particular, this was characterized by a more medically dominated approach, with public health increasingly being defined as public health medicine and community nursing moving from traditional community health nursing models to more medical models (Ashton and Seymour 1988; Ottewill and Wall 1990). This development had important implications both for the future of the disciplines involved and for the nature and extent of public participation which are addressed in the next section of this chapter. However, before doing so we need to consider the impact of those aspects of the reforms implemented in 1974 which aimed to increase public participation.

## Statutory mechanisms for public involvement

One feature of the 1974 reforms was the establishment of the post of Health Services Commissioner (HSC) – the ombudsman for health. This move resulted from concerns about the treatment of individual patients within the NHS. The role and remit of the HSC, however, was constrained in many ways. Most importantly, its jurisdiction was confined to non-clinical areas – a perceived limitation by many patient groups as most complaints related to clinical practice (Hogg 1995) – and the opportunity for involvement was limited insofar as the Commissioner could only act after the event. The NHS complainant had to be tenacious as complaints had first to go through the normal procedures before they could be dealt with by the HSC. As Boaden *et al* (1982) remark, moreover, the formal nature of the procedures involved meant that inevitably they would tend to be used mainly by the articulate and well-informed patient. In terms of public involvement, therefore, the key element of the 1974 reforms was the establishment of the Community Health Councils (CHCs). Located in each district health authority with a brief to represent the consumer interest, the development of CHCs appeared initially to resolve the problem of local accountability.

From the beginning, however, the CHCs experienced problems with their constitution and their ability to act as agents of the public (Klein and Lewis 1976); there was substantial ambiguity about who the CHCs would represent and how that representation would be effected. Klein and Lewis (1976) consider that, while the resultant membership of the CHC – one-third local authority representatives, one-third regional NHS appointees and one-third elected by voluntary organizations – appeared to meet all relevant political interests, the key issue of representation was essentially left unresolved. Klein (1995) has argued that one of the roles of CHCs was to further the sectional interests of particular groups of service users, namely people with learning disabilities, people with mental health problems and elderly people. This is reflected in the emphasis on these groups in the voluntary sector constituency of the CHCs. The role of the councils, however, as an avenue for wider public or local accountability has never been wholly clear, except perhaps in some limited fashion through their local authority representation.

In part, the difficulties faced by the CHCs were due to the absence of explicit policy objectives or a strong legislative framework within which to operate. In part it was the result of the lack of resources available to undertake the broad range of duties and services expected of them (Longley 1993; Klein 1995). The outcome has been that individual CHCs have developed very different sets of activities and priorities (Lupton *et al.* 1995). Generally, however, the CHCs have emphasized their statutory commitment to pursue complaints, undertake provider visits and monitor changes in healthcare provision. While these activities are of value as processes of accountability, they typically relate to individuals rather than communities. Coupled with their inadequate funding, moreover, this focus on provider issues has meant that the CHCs found it difficult to address wider healthcare issues. How far this situation remains today will be examined in Chapter 7 where the relationship between CHCs and healthcare commissioners is considered in more detail.

Following the 1972 local government and 1974 NHS reforms, the Government urged closer cooperation between health and local authorities, especially social services departments. During the late 1970s, joint planning machinery was set up at member level (the Joint Consultative Committee (JCC)) and at officer level to '. . . take into account and integrate with local authority plans for social services, environmental health, housing, education and transport. The aim is for comprehensive planning on a wide front to produce effective joint plans for interdependent services' (DHSS 1976). In its early stages, the machinery was simply a formal mechanism for bringing together the relevant organizations. However, in 1982 three voluntary sector members were included on the JCC and, during the 1980s, most areas developed joint planning structures which gradually involved the voluntary sector. Much has been written about the efficacy of joint planning in the 1970s and 1980s (Booth 1979; Webb and Wistow 1986; Wistow and Brooks 1988) which we do not need to reproduce here. It is clear however that, although limited, the process provided an important avenue for involving a broader range of people through the inclusion of the voluntary sector, despite the enormous organizational, representational and practical difficulties which were part and parcel of the process (McGrath 1989).

More important perhaps, in terms of developments within the voluntary sector, was the impact of the care group structure which characterized the joint planning arrangements in most health authorities. The identification of care groups – typically those for mental health, physical disability, learning disability, elderly and children and families – served to focus the activities of voluntary groups in similar ways. In turn, this influenced the formation of user groups in the 1970s and 1980s as fora involving users and voluntary organizations in many areas fed into the joint planning groups and began similarly to centre their debates around care group patterns. Despite greater opportunities for involvement, however, these years were marked by a growing dissatisfaction on the part of voluntary organizations and user representatives about the quality of the NHS and its responsiveness to their concerns and interests. The 1960s witnessed a series of major public scandals about the quality of care provided to elderly people and those with mental health problems (Robb 1967; DHSS 1969).

The years up to the 1980s thus saw a number of attempts to 'square the circle' and address the inherent dichotomies that were established within the NHS at its inception. The original tensions between central–local and professional–managerial control surfaced in many ways. The desire to impose a coherent national framework on the service led to increasing centralization, for example, which raised important issues about the extent and nature of local democratic control. In turn, questions of central accountability and rational management were raised by attempts to improve local responsiveness through CHCs and complaints procedures. The continued existence of these basic tensions within the NHS led to a preoccupation on the part of successive governments with the development of strategic objectives and the examination of the management and structure of the service (Edwards 1995). Within months of the 1974 reorganization, the then Labour Government launched yet another Royal Commission on the health service only to report to the new Conservative Government in 1979 (DHSS 1979). By then new ideas about the organization and delivery of public services were proliferating as politicians reacted to the economic and social difficulties of the mid and late 1970s. At the same time, new approaches to addressing community health needs were beginning to develop alongside a growing voluntary and community sector with a health and social care focus. These developments were to intersect in the 1980s.

## The 1980s: the introduction of general management and the rediscovery of public health

The 1980s saw a dramatic rise in the number of complaints about primary care and hospital treatment, both through the normal procedures and to the Health Services Commissioner. While it is not clear whether this situation reflected a deterioration in the service or a growing willingness to complain (or both), the increased volume of complaints suggests that the NHS was not meeting the expectations of its patients. Klein (1995) has argued that the growth in private health insurance over the same period must be seen as a further indication that the NHS was failing to respond to the needs of the public. In this sense we can identify a difference between continuing public support for the NHS in general and more specific problems arising from the actual operation of the service. As we have seen, however, there was little institutional concern with the notion of responsibility to patients or the wider public; for those managing the service, the central line of accountability was upward to the Secretary of State and through him or her to parliament.

In the early 1980s the newly elected Conservative Government again attempted to address the perceived organizational problems of the NHS, driven partly by an ideological concern to reduce the size and cost of the public sector (see Chapter 3). The subsequent reforms of the NHS in 1982 were thus prompted by the need to decrease the levels of bureaucracy and to increase the extent of managerial control exerted by the regional health authorities. The prime aim of the district health boards was to manage the service, with the concept of local representation being kept alive through their local authority representatives. In this way, Klein (1995) sees the reforms as again trying to reach an appropriate compromise between the competing pressures of central and local accountability, on the one hand, and managerial and professional control on the other. However, this time it is significant that the reform of the NHS was taking place in the context of a much broader process of managerial change characterizing the whole of the public sector.

The introduction of the new public managerialism into the NHS was spearheaded by the 1983 Griffiths Report. As we have seen, the central objective of this report was to engender a shift in the organizational focus of the service from the administration of healthcare to the management of healthcare. Griffiths was highly critical of the consensus management approach adopted in 1974 and of the insularity of NHS managers. The underlying thrust of his report was to increase managerial control over doctors in part by drawing the latter into management themselves (Ranade 1995). The recurring themes of Griffiths' managerialism were energy and efficiency, effective budgeting, sensitivity to consumers and an approach to personnel management which rewards good performance and threatens poor performance with dismissal (Cox 1991).

One area on which the new general managers were encouraged to place greater emphasis was that of attending to consumer preferences. The reference to broader public involvement within the report, however, was fairly vague (Harrison and Pollitt 1994), referring only to a basic lack of knowledge about whether the service was delivering what the public wanted: '. . . whether the NHS is meeting the needs of the patients and the community, and can prove that it is doing so is open to question' (DHSS 1983: 10). While the 1980s saw the growth of mechanisms for identifying consumer satisfaction by hospitals and health authorities (McIvor 1991), it is debatable how effective these were as methods of obtaining user views. In their study of the implementation of general management in the NHS, Strong and Robinson (1990) conclude that overall the reforms militated against increased consumer involvement. In particular, the health authority boards became more concerned with implementing national agendas than with developing priorities in consultation with local communities.

At the same time as the NHS was focusing on the new managerialism and exploring consumerist approaches, wider influences relating to a renewed interest in public health were beginning to develop in the UK, having their roots in the values of the community health and new public health movements (Ashton and Seymour 1988). A key element of these approaches was the emphasis on community participation and collaboration. As with the user movements proliferating at the same time, the relationship between the community health movement and the NHS progressed in a complex fashion with the impetus for development coming from both within and outside the NHS. Although at times attracting the support of the NHS and its workers, community health initiatives were often relegated to the margins of healthcare.

### Community health initiatives

Community health action developed in the late 1970s with six community health projects set up in the UK in 1977 by the Foundation for Alternatives. These were short-term funded neighbourhood health initiatives and all but one failed to survive beyond the first year of funding (Scott-Samuel 1989). Despite being neighbourhood initiatives, Scott-Samuel has argued that this failure was due to their not being sufficiently rooted in the local community. From these beginnings a number of initiatives subsequently developed, focused either on geographical communities or neighbourhoods such as the Stockwell Health Project (Kenner 1986) or on communities of interest such as the Avon Vietnamese Refugee Community Project and the Lambeth Women and Children's Health Project (Dun 1991).

Dun (1991) argues that the fundamental aspect of community health initiatives is that they are self-determining, developing their own view of health needs and how they should be met. For Rosenthal (1983), similarly, the key characteristic of the community health movement is that it is based firmly outside the health professions. In the early 1980s this movement continued to develop through the establishment of the London Community Health Resource (1981) and the Community Health Initiatives Resource Unit (1983). These organizations merged in 1988 to form the National Community Health Resource. By the mid 1980s there were thousands of local health groups across the country (Kenner 1986). These groups were often totally independent from healthcare services but in many cases worked alongside or with community and primary healthcare workers and healthcare professionals in hospitals. It is not possible within the confines of this book to chart the growth and range of these groups, which has been undertaken extensively elsewhere (Rosenthal 1983; Kenner 1986; Dun 1991; Public Health Alliance 1991). However, there are important implications for healthcare decision making arising from the experiences of community health initiatives which have a direct bearing on issues of healthcare purchasing. Of particular interest is the extent to which such groups and initiatives have been able to influence healthcare decision-making processes.

The community health approach has been widely supported in the development of the new public health and the 'Healthy City' and 'Health for All' movements (Ashton and Seymour 1988). The principles of participation, which were made explicit in the World Health Organization's 'Health for All 2000', focused on the role of the community working with healthcare professionals (WHO 1985). Yet this policy was never given the formal support of the UK government and, while the 'Health for All' movement grew steadily in the 1980s, (Scott-Samuel 1989) there was no universal adoption of the approach across the country. The community health movement was also rooted in the democratic/citizen philosophy of participation and the real level of participation in formalized 'Healthy City/Health for All' projects was often very low and not achieved without considerable difficulties (Petersen 1996). The focus on community or place – an approach advocated by proponents of the new public health (Ashton and Seymour 1988) – found some support in the NHS with experiments with PATCH (Planned Approach or Primary Action Towards Community Health) in places such as Pimlico and Lambeth (Dun 1989).

The community health movement also increasingly presented a challenge to the Government's policy in the 1980s with its emphasis on self-defined needs and recognition of the broader environmental, material and social bases of inequalities in health (DHSS *et al.* 1980; Townsend *et al.* 1987; Thunhurst 1991). Equity was a key plank of 'Health for All' and also of the community health movement. However, the Government and the NHS did not take on this broader perspective of health. For example, Edwina Currie, the then Minister for Health, commented on the Black Report: 'I honestly don't think [health] has anything to do with poverty. The problem very often for many people is just ignorance . . . and failing to realise they do have some control over their own lives' (quoted in Townsend 1990: 383). This individualistic approach to the public's health was formally reflected in *The Health of the Nation* (DoH 1992) which emphasized the importance of personal lifestyle choices (Ranade 1995). Many have highlighted the complacency of the Government's response to the goals of 'Health for All', with no national strategy being developed and the issues of equity, community participation and inter sectoral working being largely ignored in its response to the WHO (Ranade 1995).

Generally then, the development of community health projects and the focus on new approaches to public health were not adopted into mainstream NHS activity. The evidence on the relationship between community health projects and the NHS is poor, but overall it would appear that such activity was marginalized and remained dependent on the goodwill of individual healthcare workers, particularly those in community health units (Ottewill and Wall 1990). Many initiatives were piecemeal and/or short-lived. The role of community and place, therefore, developed alongside the NHS rather than as a constituent part of healthcare services. What then was the experience of the developing user group movement?

### The user movement comes of age

The emergence of service user groups can be seen within the same broad movement of community health and self-help which occurred over the

1970s and comprise the 'community of interest' groups referred to by Dun (1991). Their roots, as we have seen, stretch back over a century and their subsequent development reflects the broader patterns in the growth of direct action discussed in Chapter 4. In the late 1970s and early 1980s, the proliferation of single issue/interest groups in the health field reflected not only an increased dissatisfaction with the delivery of healthcare services, which had driven the development of health-related groups since the 1960s, but also a concern to influence healthcare decision making directly (Boaden *et al.* 1982). In addition, there was also a growing disaffection on the part of user groups with the claim of the broader voluntary sector to speak on their behalf (Lindow 1993).

Three specific movements can be identified as contributing to the development of user groups: theories of normalization; increased self-determination among users associated with acquiring rights; and the growth of the advocacy movement. The theory of normalization developed alongside the more general policy shift from institutional to community-based care, perhaps epitomised in this country by the King's Fund's work on learning disability in the early 1980s (Towell 1988). The 'Ordinary Life' programme emphasized the citizenship rights of people with a learning disability – the right to an ordinary life rather than one segregated from society (Towell 1988; Towell and Beardshaw 1991). Thus, the corollary to normalization is the need for opportunities and mechanisms for reflecting the views of people, to recognize their right to have a say about their healthcare and to acquire the rights of citizens (Winn 1990). Since the 1950s, the dominant theme has been for people with mental health problems, learning and physical disabilities to live as independent a life as possible in the community. The most explicit recognition of this policy was contained in *Caring for People* (DoH *et al.* 1989b), the Government's response to the Griffiths' Report on community care (Griffiths 1988). The growth in self-determination reflects the idea of normalization but also comes from within the user movement. It involves a commitment to the process of self-realization and to the assertion of democratic rights as well as to the rise of self-advocacy.

Self-advocacy grew throughout the 1980s with strong roots in the areas of mental health, physical disability and learning disability. The development of organizations of mental health users such as Survivors Speak Out, Link in Glasgow and the Women and Mental Health Network in Bristol provided radical alternatives to traditional approaches to involving users in the 1980s. Essentially self-advocacy is concerned with sharing power with users of services (Whittaker 1989; Winn 1990). While the concept of sharing power is also central to the citizen advocacy movement there is a different emphasis. Citizen advocacy involves the use of citizens to befriend and act as advocates of people who require support to speak for themselves (Sang 1984). The concept of citizen advocacy comes from North America, with the movement in the UK developing from the disability movement and finding its formal 'coming of age' with the establishment of the Advocacy Alliance in 1982 – set up by MIND, MENCAP, One-to-One,

the Spastics Society and the Leonard Cheshire Foundation. Thus in relation to the user movement there are perhaps three key elements: self-
determination, self-advocacy and citizen advocacy. The essential unifying
features are the emphasis on users' right to have control over their lives
(the acquisition of citizenship) and the commitment to power sharing with
professionals so that users may have a say in decisions that affect their lives.

To an extent, the growth of the user movement has involved a process
of assimilation between patient and illness specific organizations and
healthcare professionals. This has led to a reticence on behalf of some
health managers to deal with user groups on the basis that they do not
represent the real views of service users as much as platforms for health
professionals. While it may be simplistic, such a view was an important
factor in the growing desire among healthcare managers to make contact
with 'real' healthcare users directly. This occurred at the same time as
users themselves were actively questioning the right of voluntary organizations to represent their interests. The focus on ascertaining the direct views
of individual users was further stimulated by the consumerist approaches
of the new managerialism within the NHS, driven both by the desire to
curb the power of the professionals and to scrutinize the performance of
managers (see Chapter 2).

## New solutions for old problems?

As we have argued throughout this chapter, the policy goal within the
NHS has mainly been to address the inherent tensions arising from the
different and competing demands of professional autonomy, the principles
of rational management and the need to balance central and local control.
There is little evidence in the first thirty years of the NHS of any significant interest in public or patient involvement, with the exception of the
development of CHCs and the establishment of complaints procedures.
The extent of public involvement provided by these initiatives, moreover,
was limited. The CHCs were established to represent sectional interests
rather than to serve as a vehicle for wider public involvement; elections to
the Councils involved only one-third of their members and were confined
to representatives of recognized and registered voluntary organizations.
The operation of the complaints system was restricted to issues of
maladministration, leaving matters relating to the quality of care under the
auspices of professional regulating bodies. It was only towards the end of
the 1970s, and the growth of voluntary sector involvement in joint planning in the early 1980s in particular, that the NHS was beginning to
recognize the need to involve community organizations and the wider
public. Even here we find that opportunities were limited as participation
in the joint planning processes required involvement in the local voluntary
sector and depended on the effectiveness of arrangements for consultation
between voluntary groups. As Wistow (1990) has commented, the lack of
a voluntary infrastructure in many areas of the country militated against

such coordination. Generally in these years, therefore, wider public involvement from an institutional perspective was limited to the democratic processes of central government elections or local authority nominations to the CHCs and health boards.

The growth of the user movement in the late 1980s and, in particular, the debate about representation which took place within the broader voluntary sector, had significant implications for the development of public involvement in the 1990s. Significantly, this coincided with a growing interest in the notion of consumerism within the NHS itself. Concerns about accountability in the NHS had continued to plague much of the discussion at local and national level and, as Strong and Robinson (1990) demonstrate in their study of the district health authorities in the late 1980s, were of real and growing importance to many working within the NHS. One of the main objectives of the Griffiths' reforms was to engender a more consumer-orientated approach to healthcare. Combined with the emphasis on quality which emerged in the wake of the NHS management reforms, the idea of consulting with service users was proving increasingly attractive to policy makers and service providers alike.

The interest in consumerism coincided with the three key developments in public involvement discussed above: the growth of interest groups challenging the ability of bureaucracies to provide appropriate services; the concern about professionals having sole responsibility for providing care; and the growth of user and carer groups articulating common and individual interests (Williamson 1992). The framework for consumer interests was thus laid prior to the introduction of the internal market in the NHS. At the same time, broader principles of public participation were being developed through joint planning mechanisms and community health movements.

In one sense, the growth of consumer and interest groups in health provided a response to the inability of the NHS to provide a broad accountability framework beyond the centralist model and the democratic process. To an extent, this problem was shared by all major public institutions and had been under discussion for a number of years with the issue of representation being hotly debated (Gyford 1991). The introduction of the internal market within the NHS in 1991, however, further eroded the institutionalized opportunities for public involvement. The removal of local authority nominations from health authority boards, and the abolition of the old regional structure and boards reduced the opportunities for members of the public to become involved in healthcare services. In addition the growth of general practice fundholding (GPFH) and total purchasing, means that many decisions about the commissioning of healthcare services have been removed from the public to the professional domain. Chapter 6 examines in greater depth the implications of the introduction of the NHS internal market for the relationship between commissioning and public involvement.

# 6 Healthcare purchasing: a new framework for public involvement

## Introduction

From Chapter 5 it can be seen that the discussion of public participation has traditionally focused on the delivery of healthcare and has primarily addressed the involvement of people in the services they receive. This service perspective has also permeated the theoretical discussion of participation (see for example Richardson 1983; Hallett 1987). Since the NHS and Community Care Act 1990, however, there has been a growing interest in public participation in social care services – particularly given the requirement to involve users in the community care planning process – and in purchasing, as well as the provision of services (NHSME 1992; NAHAT 1994). The framework for purchasing was established in the 1989 White Paper *Working for Patients* (DoH 1989a) which set out new arrangements for an internal market in healthcare. Central to the development of the internal market was the separation of purchasers (DHAs and GP fundholders) from the providers of healthcare services (community trusts, hospitals, private and independent provision). While such changes built on the management reforms of the 1980s, the internal market changed the whole context of the relationship between the NHS and the public. Initially, the focus of government policy was on the development of the providers but after 1993 there was an increasing focus on the role of purchasers generally and the role of GPs in particular. This emphasis was maintained by the new Labour Government elected in 1997, with its proposals for locality commissioning.

Under the proposals contained in the White Paper, and enacted by the NHS and Community Care Act, purchasers were required to buy health services on behalf of their local populations or, in the case of the GP fundholders, their practice patients. The new role of the purchaser as the agent of the public has led to a shift in the debate about public involvement in the NHS, with an increased emphasis on functional issues relating to the assessment of need, priority setting and service review (NHSME 1993; NAHAT 1993; Øvretveit 1995). There has also been a greater concern with the broader political questions of responsibility and accountability, partly derived from the growth of debates about governance over the early 1990s (Cairncross and Ashburner 1992; Longley 1993). These discussions have taken place within the citizen/democratic and consumer/ market dichotomy of public involvement described in earlier chapters and have been affected by ongoing organizational changes to the service such as the merging of district health authorities (DHAs) and the family health services authorities (FHSAs) and the move to a primary care-led NHS.

While the development of purchasing in healthcare has been well documented (Prowle 1992; Glennerster *et al.* 1994; Saltman and von Otter 1995; Øvretveit 1995; Ham 1996), there has been little attempt to examine the issue in relation to public involvement, despite its obvious implications for the context in which that involvement takes place. In beginning this task, this chapter provides a detailed discussion of the development of purchasing within the NHS following the introduction of the internal market in 1991. The implications of the organizational development of the purchasing function for issues of accountability and responsibility are then examined in the context of the democratic and consumerist perspectives discussed previously. The chapter concludes by considering the extent to which and ways in which the changing policy context and organization of healthcare purchasing has resulted in the search for new frameworks for public accountability and for new ways of involving people in healthcare services.

## The development of purchasing

Purchasing was introduced into the NHS by the White Paper *Working for Patients* (DoH *et al.* 1989a) with similar principles being applied to social care in the later White Paper on community care, *Caring for People* (DoH *et al.* 1989b). The proposals, involving the separation of the purchaser and provider function, were implemented in April 1991, following the NHS and Community Care Act 1990. The Act established two types of health purchasers – the district health authorities (DHAs) and the GP fundholders (GPFHs). The responsibility of the DHA shifted from the planning and management of healthcare services to the strategic responsibility for assessing need, setting priorities, allocating resources and contracting for services. At first considered marginal, the GPFH mode of purchasing was to develop substantially over the years of the mid 1990s.

This bifurcation of purchasing resulted in the development of two different approaches which have been described as 'population-centred purchasing' and 'patient-focused purchasing' (Ham 1996). Although the main discussion of this book is on the development of public involvement and population-centred purchasing within the health authority context, it is impossible to ignore the increasing impact of GP-based, patient-focused purchasing, or fundholding as it is more commonly known. The establishment of 'total purchasing' projects in 1995, with groups of fundholders holding the full budget for their practice populations, added a further dimension. In addition, a wide variety of hybrid purchasing systems developed incorporating elements of both these approaches. The policy of the incoming Labour Government has been to dismantle some of the key elements of the internal market, although retaining the purchaser–provider split and supporting primary care-led purchasing via the establishment of Primary Care Groups (DoH 1997b).

Purchasing was to be one of the key activities of DHAs and those GP practices which became fundholders. Initially, however, there was scant official guidance provided on the development of purchasing which, together with an initial requirement for 'steady-state' contracts with providers, afforded little stimulus for purchasers to focus on their role. In fact, the main policy emphasis in the years immediately following the 1990 Act was on provider development and the creation of Trust status. As Prowle (1992) and Ham (1994) have argued, in the early years of the internal market purchasers, of necessity, focused on contractual or short-term purchasing issues which addressed the nature and efficiency of current service patterns and the political imperatives of waiting lists. It was not until 1993 that the DoH and NHSME specifically addressed purchasing with a succession of speeches by the then Minister for Health, Brian Mawhinney and the Chief Executive of the NHS, Duncan Nichol (NHSME 1993). These speeches followed a period of increased interest in the role of purchasing with regional reviews of purchasing being undertaken during the previous year (Ham and Spurgeon 1992; Hunter and Harrison 1993). The reviews provided conflicting views of the purposes of purchasing and the role of purchasers.

What is clear from these reviews of purchasing is that the internal market in the NHS cannot function like a normal market where there is a direct contract between the user of services and the provider of services. This is a recognized feature of internal or 'quasi' markets (Mullen 1990) where the purchaser of the services (the DHA) is not the same as the consumer of services (the patient) (Le Grand and Bartlett 1993). Achieving the goals for patient choice and responsiveness set out in the White Papers thus requires the development of mechanisms which create links between purchasers and service users. While the concept of 'consumer responsiveness' is seen as a key aspect of the market relationship, in the context of the NHS (and other public services) this occurs only indirectly; in the main, it is the purchaser who relates directly to the provider through contracts made on the public's behalf. This tripartite relationship is crucial to understanding how their functional responsibilities within the internal market necessitates an interest on the part of purchasers in involving the public more directly. In order to explore this issue more fully, it is important to examine the subsequent development of the purchasing role.

The 1992 regional reviews noted the strong emphasis on contracting issues and little on the development of strategic purchasing, which Prowle (1992) has described as the consideration of what services the health authority should be purchasing to meet local health needs and how, and from whom, it should purchase. Empirical work on purchasing, such as that undertaken by Klein *et al.* (1996) on reviewing purchasing plans, has confirmed the lack of strategic attention and the fact that '. . . most health authorities are only gradually, and incrementally, modifying the inherited variations in the pattern of services' (Klein 1995: 233). While the language of purchasing, particularly in the initial policy documents, has been informed by market approaches – such as achieving efficiency through competition – the practice of purchasing has emphasized issues of collaboration and sustained relationships between purchasers and providers. This is an important issue as often the language of purchasing differs substantively from the process, with important implications for public involvement. This divergence between process and language may also reflect subsequent shifts in terminology from 'purchasing' as the key description of the role of purchasers to that of 'commissioning', with a distinction being drawn between 'strategic' and 'operational' purchasing.

The use of the term 'commissioning' in connection with health authority purchasers, particularly following the merging of DHAs and FHSAs, originated in the former Wessex Region in 1994 and was gradually extended across the country. The mergers were formally adopted nationally with the establishment, in 1996, of 100 new health authorities under the Health Authorities Act 1995. However, there was no consensus on the definition of either purchasing or commissioning, with the two terms often being used interchangeably. Some commentators argue that purchasing relates more to operational or short-term elements such as contracting and that commissioning represents the longer-term, more strategic element of the purchasing process (Øvretveit 1995; Robinson and Le Grand 1995). Although this distinction appears to have been recognized in the development of the commissioning role of the new health authorities, it was not shared by the NHSE (1994) which continued to describe long-term strategic approaches as purchasing. Subsequently, the term 'commissioning' was used in connection with GP or locality commissioning – an approach favoured by the incoming Labour Government in 1997. While there may have been no agreement over the concepts of commissioning and purchasing, a broad commonality of purpose can be identified:

The main purpose of the current [1991] reforms of the NHS is to create a new regime of competition between purchasers and providers of health care services. The goal is underpinned by basic objectives of facilitating greater consumer/patient choice and promoting efficiency in resource allocation and use. Purchasers are required to define their priorities through a process of health needs assessment and a local strategy for maximising 'health gain'. This will then inform their selection of appropriate providers and determine the kinds of contracts placed.

(Flynn *et al.* 1995: 530)

For Flynn *et al.* (1995), contracts are the key mechanism through which purchasers achieve such objectives. This view is supported by Robinson and Le Grand (1995). Yet contracting is only one element of the purchasing or commissioning process which has framed purchasers' approaches to public involvement. While this may have been the focus of purchaser activity in the early years of the internal market, it is clear that the emphasis placed on developing purchasers in 1993 (NHSME 1993) was about developing strategy and a more robust purchasing process. Assessments of purchasing in these early years show that the core functions of purchasing organizations became clearer through experience and that the process was becoming more complex with the development of strategic functions such as needs assessment, collaborating with other agencies, involving GPs and developing strategic plans (Carruthers *et al.* 1995). These experiences echo the seven 'stepping stones' to effective purchasing set out by Dr Mawhinney, the Minister for Health in 1993 – a strategic view, effective contracts, a sound knowledge base, responsiveness to local people, mature relations between purchasers and providers, local alliances and organizational capacity (NHSME 1993).

As suggested above, crucial to the understanding of purchasing is the concept of the purchasing process or purchasing cycle. The cycle is shown in Figure 6.1. The various stages of the cycle are usually understood to

**Figure 6.1** The purchasing cycle.

be sequential and relate to the yearly NHS contracting round between purchasers and providers. In practice, the stages are not wholly sequential, and the whole process is more complex than Figure 6.1 suggests. In relation to public involvement, the cycle was explicitly used to structure the discussions in *Local Voices* (NHSME 1992) and Chapter 7 draws on this framework to discuss health authority experiences of public involvement.

More importantly, as has already been referred to, the development of purchasing has not been uniform, with the contracting element of the cycle being developed first and other elements of the cycle being slower to emerge. Redmayne (1996), who has reviewed health authority purchasing plans over a number of years, reported that the development of purchasing has been an evolutionary process rather than one characterized by dramatic change. Health authority purchasers have gradually refined the purchasing process within the constraints of centrally determined policy (Flynn *et al.* 1996; Ham 1996) and, as Redmayne (1996: 31) has identified: 'Whatever their aspirations and ambitions, the dictates of financial and organizational feasibility have constrained their scope for change.'

For health authorities to adopt a population-centred approach to purchasing, the development of needs assessment to identify what health services are required is fundamental. It is from this that strategic purchasing intentions are generated and annual purchasing plans formulated. Key to this has been the development of public health and the publishing of annual public health plans identifying health needs. Strategy development is the next stage of the purchasing cycle and requires the identification of long-term healthcare strategies on which annual purchasing plans can be based. In a study of the reforms in four case studies in the West Midlands, Appleby (1994) found that this strategic capacity was developing only very slowly:

> Purchasers were still trying to get to grips with the basic information they required to assess health care needs and make rational decisions concerning choice of provider – based on quantifiable measures of quality, reliable data on prices and, importantly, *local opinion*. But in addition, purchasers are only just beginning to grapple with the underlying methodologies of priority setting, the construction of contracts and the information implications of monitoring contract performance.
> (Appleby 1994: 47; emphasis added)

While health authorities have been slow to develop strategic health policy, the preparation and publication of annual purchasing plans has been a cornerstone of health authority activity (Redmayne 1996). The plan is a statement of purchasing intentions for a single financial year and has to be formally consulted upon with other agencies. The focus of attention on purchasing plans may also have helped emphasize the contracting part of the process as current patterns of provision formed the basis of purchasing in the early years. This emphasis may have also been due to the central place of contracts as a mechanism for ensuring healthcare services delivery.

Generally, service contracts were placed in line with historical service patterns. The aspiration to develop more appropriate services was clearly identified by purchasing managers in the early years of the market (Appleby *et al.* 1994) and the research on purchasing community health services by Flynn *et al.* (1996) supports the view that purchasers are moving towards an increasing emphasis on contracting for outcomes and health gain. This clearly demonstrates the development of a more strategic approach to purchasing by health authorities. It also suggests that health authorities may be taking the issue of monitoring and evaluation more seriously.

Of particular interest to the discussion here is the gradual development from contracting to strategic health purchasing which demanded more complex information about local needs and views. While clearly identified as a policy priority in documents such as *Local Voices* (NHSME 1992), the involvement of local people also arose from the operational aspects of purchasing. The need to develop more sophisticated methods of needs assessment, identifying priorities and reviewing services, required methods for gaining public views. Redmayne (1996) found that public consultation was a key theme of purchasing plans, with an emphasis on disseminating information and gathering local views. The importance of these activities is also noted in case studies of purchasing (Carruthers *et al.* 1995; Flynn *et al.* 1996). The ability of health authority purchasers to address these issues is explored fully in Chapter 7.

Much of the development of the purchasing process has been highly dependent on organizational capacity and the ability to undertake a purchasing function. Notwithstanding the continuous organizational change which has affected health authorities over the past few years, through mergers and reductions in the management overheads, the task of purchasing is still fairly new and skills are still developing (Carruthers *et al.* 1995; Flynn *et al.* 1996; Redmayne 1996). There has, despite the regional reviews, been no real blueprint for what an effective purchaser should look like. This was an issue which faced the Audit Commission in its review of the development of fundholding (Audit Commission 1996). While there has been an increasing focus on needs assessment, strategy development and priority setting, monitoring progress and evaluating outcomes, the performance of purchasers in these processes has been variable in approach, organization and achievement (Redmayne 1996). Purchasing development has been fragmented and dependent on local approaches despite national guidelines and strong central policy direction in terms of priorities for action through the NHS planning documents. In turn, as Appleby *et al.* (1994) and others have argued, the ability of purchasers to react to local issues has been severely limited due to centrally driven priorities such as *The Patient's Charter* and waiting lists.

With the increasing development of primary care, or patient-centred, purchasing and a primary care-led NHS, the issue of defining commissioning and purchasing became linked to the distinctive roles of primary and health authority purchasers. This is an issue to which we will return later, insofar as the distinction is important to an understanding of the role of public involvement, but it is important here to review the development of primary care-based purchasing to provide some context for these later discussions.

## The rise of primary care-based purchasing

The gradual re-emergence of the role of primary care has been one of the key trends since the mid 1980s. The establishment of the NHS in 1948 placed a central focus on the role and importance of hospitals, with GPs having a semi-independent status. Since the late 1970s and early 1980s, culminating in the Green Paper *Promoting Better Health* (DHSS 1987) and re-emphasized in *Working for Patients* (DoH *et al.* 1989a), the role for primary care has been more clearly mapped out. Interest in primary care has emanated from the desire to control access to expensive acute-based healthcare via the gatekeeper role of GPs and from concerns about the lack of control over the demand-led expenditure of general practice. GP fundholding, the 1991 contract and the development of 'total fundholding', can all be seen to have developed from these concerns (Glennerster *et al.* 1994).

Any discussion about the future direction of primary healthcare services is now firmly entwined with the development of primary care led purchasing (NHSE 1994, 1996a; DoH 1996c; DoH 1997b). This initiative has seen a remarkable move onto the political and policy agenda since its inception in the late 1980s as GP fundholding and its relatively minor role in *Working for Patients*. Fundholding, and its derivatives, has increasingly been seen as one of the key forces for change within the reformed NHS. Advocates of fundholding talk about its closeness to the patient, its patient-focused approach to purchasing, the freedom for GPs to provide better services for their patients and to influence patterns of provision by community and acute units (Glennerster *et al.* 1994).

Despite the equivocal nature of the research evidence concerning its success (Coulter 1995; Stewart-Brown *et al.* 1996), since its inception in 1991 fundholding quickly extended in scope – with 53 pilot total fundholding projects being established by 1997 – and, with the reduction in list size and the concept of community fundholding, has encompassed increasing numbers of GPs (NHSE 1994). It is clear that the scheme, which was included in *Working for Patients* at the last minute to provide a more radical edge to the reforms, not only created a substantial amount of controversy (Whitehead 1994; Coulter 1995) but also fundamentally changed patterns of service delivery in some areas of healthcare (Glennerster *et al.* 1994; Audit Commission 1996).

Key questions about the efficiency and effectiveness of fundholding however remain to be answered (Coulter 1995; Dixon and Glennerster 1995), in particular those concerning the 'transaction costs' of setting up and monitoring contracts and patient care – an issue only partly addressed in the Audit Commission report (1996). These costs would seem to be high because of the individualized nature of general practice and it remains to be seen whether they can be restrained by the development of primary care commissioning and different forms of contracting. What is not in question is the fact that fundholding spearheaded a fundamental shift towards a primary care-led NHS, rooted in general practice, which is changing the nature of relationships between commissioners and the community. The assumption that GPs are closer to the community has, as we have seen, led many DHAs to use them as proxies for public views on healthcare (Klein *et al.* 1996). While this may be appropriate, to an extent, in respect of individual patient experiences, and as an indicator of public 'ill-health needs', it is not at all clear that GPs are the most effective representatives of the broader healthcare views of communities (Heritage 1994; Neeve 1994). In fact, the available evidence on primary care and public involvement, which indicates that GPs do not adequately communicate with their patients, raises questions about their capability and/or inclination adequately to reflect the needs of their practice populations (Agass *et al.* 1991; Brown 1994).

The operation of general practice is based on GPs and other healthcare professionals meeting the needs of patients who have demanded and sought healthcare services. This highly individualized view of healthcare may serve to reinforce consumerist methods of involvement and distance more collective approaches. While many authorities have attempted to develop locality-based approaches drawing together groups of GPs – an approach encapsulated in the idea of Primary Care Groups (DoH 1997b) – it is also clear that many fundholders operate in a highly individualized way with a focus on particular patients. It is unlikely that these new purchasing organizations will put much effort into developing community involvement because they face many other challenges, not least the need to develop new organizational models and management structures in primary care agencies. As such, the reliance on GPs as consumer-proxies may tend to reinforce the role of the medical professional and further devalue the views of the public, creating a strong professionally dominated approach to the definition of local health issues. Ironically, thus, the reforms may lead to an enhancement of, rather than a challenge to, medical autonomy.

At the same time as these changes pose practical difficulties for public involvement, there appears to be a renewed interest in the idea with a shift in emphasis from the more functional or operational aspects of purchasing to wider issues of political accountability. While proposals made by the Conservative Government in 1996 to develop new models of primary care (DoH 1996c) and plans by the then Labour Opposition to develop mandatory, GP-led, locality commissioning arrangements (*MedEconomics* 1997) placed general practice at the centre of the commissioning process, little reference was made to the mechanisms needed to ensure the accountability of such arrangements. The new Labour Government's approach to public health and inequalities in health introduced a different emphasis, with firm pledges to dismantle the internal market but retain the purchaser–provider division being accompanied by a strong emphasis on collaboration (EL (97) 33). The proposals contained in the White Paper, *The New NHS* (DoH 1997b) which focused on drawing a wide range of players from the NHS and local government into primary care-based commissioning groups along the lines of the Total Purchasing Projects appears to be a natural progression from pre-existing collaboration between GPs and health authorities, drawing on the best elements of population and patient-based purchasing (Ham 1996). Despite the fact that the Labour Party had been calling before the election for increased accountability within the NHS, however, in government its policy on this question continues to remain unclear. The difficult issue of the accountability of purchasing arrangements has yet to be effectively addressed.

## Accountability and the democratic deficit

### Accountability

As Klein (1995) has argued, debates about accountability and its central/local dimensions, are not new. While the NHS has always been subject to central government control, with the principal line of democratic accountability being through Parliament, there has also been ongoing debate about the nature and relevance of forms of local accountability. Although not typically a primary consideration, the issue of accountability to the local community has been present in the thinking behind most service reorganizations. Concern about the lack of accountability to local populations, for example, was a key reason for establishing the Community Health Councils (CHCs) in 1974 to act as the consumer voice. In addition, changes to health authority membership in the early 1980s were designed to introduce a greater sense of 'representativeness' (Rees 1990; Klein 1995). The changes introduced by the Government at the end of the 1980s, however, were based on the argument that the managerial and representative tasks of the DHAs were essentially incompatible. How far this was the case is debatable (see Klein 1995), but the Government enforced the distinction by limiting DHAs to their managerial function and devolving the representative function to CHCs: 'The interests of the local community will continue to be represented by Community Health Councils, which act as a channel for consumer views to health authorities and FPCs' (DoH 1989a: para 8.7).

The Government did not, however, completely remove the idea of representation from the new boards. The subsequent *Briefing Pack for NHS Managers* (NHSME 1990) specifically addressed the issue in a section on the role of the non-executive members of regional and district health authorities. Although the document recognized that the non-executive director does not represent the community, in a passage on how the local views will be reflected it nevertheless implies that this is the case: '... as now, the non-executive members will be drawn from the local community, *and so have an understanding of its needs'* (NHSME 1990: para D6.4; emphasis added). This statement raises a number of issues, not least the implication of the particular choice of words:

> There are clearly some very questionable assumptions packed into the tiny word 'so'. Moreover, if [legitimate] 'needs' require some form of professional or other expert certification – a common, if far from incontestable, interpretation of the word – they certainly cannot be assimilated to community 'views', however expressed.
>
> (Rees 1990: 7)

The plausibility of this view of the representation of community needs, however, is not clear and nor, perhaps more importantly, is the question of how the ideas of representation and local accountability fit together. In a survey of executive and non-executive health authority members, Cairncross and Ashburner (1992) found that they possessed a multiple sense of accountability. The primary accountability, however, in terms of the health authority as a whole, for executive and non-executive members, was to the local community and to the users of the service. In terms of personal accountability, non-executive members again saw themselves accountable to the local community, whereas the executive members saw themselves as primarily accountable to the chair of the authority. The authors argue, however, that this sense of accountability may be difficult to put into operation without the existence of appropriate structures:

> It is reassuring to discover that members of the new HAs appear to have a strong sense of accountability, both individually and collectively, and that this is primarily downwards to the local community and patients. What is less clear is whether the mechanisms exist to make it work . . . Without such mechanisms, it is perhaps appropriate to describe members as feeling responsible to the local community and patients, rather than accountable to them.
>
> (Cairncross and Ashburner 1992: 22)

After 1993, there was increased interest in the question of how accountability in the health service could be achieved. This followed growing concern about the roles and responsibilities of DHA board members and an acknowledgement that purchasers should have some form of responsibility to their local community. The issue was first addressed in the discussions about corporate responsibility (NHSME 1993) and in broader debates about democratic accountability (NAHAT 1993). It also derived from the purchasers' role as 'champions of the people' in that '. . . to be effective "champions of the people", [purchasers] will have to demonstrate that they are *sensitive to local views* and generate an *accountability to their populations'* (NAHAT 1993: 20; original emphasis). That this view was part of the Conservative Government's thinking was spelled out by the then Health Minister, Virginia Bottomley in the *Health Service Journal*:

HAs and their chairs need to be persuaders and leaders. They need to involve the community in the decisions they take – working, for example, with community health councils. They need to be open and accessible. This is the root of accountability. People in grey suits must have human faces.

(Virginia Bottomley *Health Services Journal* 1994: 21)

Subsequently, the NHSE (1995a) produced the *Accountability Framework* for GP fundholding practices, which reflected the new emphasis on the development of primary care-led purchasing. The document identified four areas of clinical, financial, management and public accountability. The focus of public accountability is on providing information, involving patients in service planning and review and developing a complaints system. Together with the publication of *Patient Partnership* (NHSE 1996a) and the White Paper *Delivering the Future* (DoH 1996c), this served to refocus attention on the operational context of public involvement. Moreover, unlike *Local Voices*, (NHSME 1992) the emphasis was more firmly placed on the individual patient and his/her relationship with healthcare providers and purchasers. This, as we shall explore in later chapters, had important implications for the future development of public involvement in the NHS.

## The democratic deficit

Unlike local government, health authorities, as we have seen, lack any direct democratic mechanisms for linking with their local communities. The absence of such mechanisms, it has been argued, may give rise to perceptions of a 'democratic deficit' on the part of purchasers (Redmayne 1992). This perception may be heightened by changes to purchasers' organizational status within the post-reform NHS. Laffin (1986) draws a distinction between what he defines as the 'public service' professions (those in the front line of the service in contact with the public) and 'technobureaucratic' professions (those concerned with managing the organizations within which the 'public service' professions are employed). Within the NHS, he argues, health authority purchasers represent the 'technobureaucratic' professions, remote from the public apart from the limited local lay representation on the boards. As organizations responsible for the healthcare of their public, however, they may need to re-establish the links which may in the past have been forged through direct service provision via the 'public service' professions. This objective derives both from an operational desire to ensure that decisions are made with the best information possible and a political requirement for improved accountability to, or at least as Cairncross and Ashburner (1992) have shown, responsibility for, the local population.

One of the reasons why HAs have an interest in being seen to consult with their 'public' may therefore be to legitimize their actions, particularly so following the introduction of the purchaser/provider division. Thus

*Local Voices* (NHSME 1992) suggests that being responsive to local views will serve to enhance the credibility of health authorities. This was reinforced by the then Minister for Health in 1994, Dr Brian Mawhinney, who identified the 'need to establish local legitimacy for their priorities' as one of the key reasons for seeking more public involvement in purchasing (NHSME 1994). Securing such legitimacy may be necessary to clarify and strengthen the position of purchasers within the healthcare market. Within the NHS the prevailing view of participation has typically been as a means of improving service delivery and the opportunity for doing so may be seen to be increased by bringing in community and 'consumer' views to balance those of the service providers:

> Health Authorities cannot bring about genuine, robust change without working in partnership with local people. Having support from local people for priorities and plans can give legitimacy and justification to changes in service patterns, and strengthen the negotiating position of commissioners.
>
> (Smithies 1992)

This emphasis on consultation and legitimization thus lends support to the argument that involvement is not about providing power to consumers or communities, nor about improving accountability structures *per se*. There is evidence to suggest, in fact, little commitment to a broader goal of public empowerment on the part of purchasers or a sense that their actions should be accountable to the local community (Taylor and Lupton 1995). Rather it is primarily about the harnessing of public involvement to the strategic and operational concerns of purchasing organizations and increasing the extent to which decision making can be seen to be underpinned by (some form of) public consent. As a result, the development of public involvement is perhaps inevitably beset by the differing, and potentially conflicting, expectations and agendas of key actors: politicians, officers, professionals and the public itself. As Mechanic notes:

> ... medical care involves a variety of interest groups that tend to view priorities from their own particular perspectives and interests, and it is enormously difficult to achieve a consensus. Groups are usually reluctant to yield rights and privileges that they have already exercised, and will resist significant restructuring unless it appears to do something for them.
>
> (Mechanic 1972)

Alford notes, in particular, the negative role of professional power in the face of organized community or patient groups:

> Once community groups are mobilized, they tend to conflict with each other and with the professionals in health organizations over funding, priorities, timing, sites and control. Community participation is a classic instance of the 'veto group' process leading to stalemate.
>
> (Alford 1975)

It was precisely these issues that Sir Roy Griffiths used to justify the introduction of managers in the mid 1980s (DHSS 1983; Strong and Robinson 1990; Klein 1995).

## New frameworks

The future of healthcare commissioning will involve the development of Primary Care Groups whose roles range from advising health authorities, to acting as fully fledged purchasers (NHSE 1997c). This network of purchasers effectively disperses responsibility for aspects of healthcare commissioning such as public involvement. While competition, or at least the potential for competition, was a feature of the internal market immediately post 1991, the debate now centres on cooperation and the need for longer-term contracting. What role the public will play in this developing purchaser configuration is not clear. While, as will be discussed in later chapters, health authorities are beginning to develop structural processes for gaining public views, GP purchasers have been slow to move to a commissioning framework which involves the public. Moreover, although government policy clearly places a key responsibility on GP purchasers to involve the public (NHSE 1995a), in *Delivering the Future* the emphasis, as we have seen, remains on providing information to patients and creating responsible patients (DoH 1996c).

One consequence of the fragmentation of purchasers is the increasing focus on area or 'locality' as a means of bringing agencies together, including personal social services and other local authority services (Exworthy and Peckham forthcoming). Such an approach is epitomized in joint planning arrangements (DoH 1995b) and in many of the multi-agency teams working in community-based services. However, as we have shown in the previous chapters, existing research suggests that collaboration in general practice is not very developed (Lupton and Taylor 1997). There is growing interest among health authorities in subdistrict planning and in grouping general practices into geographical areas for planning and commissioning purposes (Balogh 1996). That this interest in locality purchasing is reflected on the political stage can be shown in the proposals introduced in 1997 by the new Labour government. While the growth of community care planning has led to the development of structures for involving users, carers and voluntary organizations, often within locality-based groups, there is little current evidence of health authorities drawing on this model and few examples of GP involvement in such processes.

These issues are, however, somewhat separate from those of public accountability. Institutional approaches to accountability have tended to focus on the operational or managerial aspects of accountability, developed via consumerist mechanisms such as charters and standards and have not addressed the more complex aspects of political or public accountability discussed in previous chapters. Such approaches also tend to highlight individual medical practice and ignore more general public health issues.

The accountability proposals (NHSE 1995a) for general practice fund-holding, for example, represent a crude framework, lacking detail on the specific nature or objectives of accountability mechanisms. While there is existing practice to build upon in relation to financial, managerial and professional accountability there are few effective foundations for developing accountability to the public. In particular, there is little guidance on balancing the different forms of accountability involved in the democratic and consumerist approaches. These issues are likely to become more complex as the increasing number of general practice purchasers serves to fragment the purchasing function. The discussion of Chapter 7 indicates some of the practical difficulties faced by purchasers attempting to develop public involvement at both health authority and primary care levels.

# 7 Public involvement: health authority responses

## Introduction

The growing emphasis on consumerism over the 1980s was a central component of the new ideology of the NHS which underpinned the 1991 reforms. A key aspect of the reforms, as identified in *Working for Patients* (DoH 1989a), was that patients should be viewed as consumers in the same way as those purchasing any other commercial product. As discussed in previous chapters, this concept is not without difficulties when applied to healthcare, but the 1991 reforms marked a watershed in terms of the adoption of the language of the market place, albeit that, as Klein (1995: 238) has noted '. . . the gap between rhetoric and reality, between aspirations and actions, may still be wide'. The definition of 'the consumer', however, is ambiguous. In addition to their responsibilities to the individual patient, health purchasers are expected themselves to act as 'proxy consumers' in that they purchase healthcare services on behalf of their population. Thus in *Local Voices* (NHSME 1992), we see an emphasis on listening to the views of the wider community as well as to those of individual consumers. This chapter assesses how health authority and, more recently, primary care purchasers have discharged their role as proxy consumers and what methods they have used to discern both consumer and community views. In so doing, it draws on evidence from the research literature on commissioning and public involvement and in particular from empirical work undertaken by the authors in the former Wessex Regional Health Authority.

The mechanisms for involving the public and consumers are varied and, in many ways, build on the developments prior to 1991 outlined in Chapter 5. They are examined here in the context of the wider policy and operational frameworks of NHS purchasing and in relation to the democratic and consumerist approaches highlighted in earlier chapters. The chapter starts by exploring these contexts in relation to the central policy guidance on public involvement given to purchasers in the early 1990s. The response of purchasers, and their actual experience of developing public involvement, is then examined, using the framework of the purchasing process. The implications of both central policy guidance and purchasers' local activities for the Community Health Councils (CHCs), as the statutory 'voice' of the patient, are also considered. Given the policy shift towards primary care purchasing, with the development of fundholding and locality commissioning, the last section of the chapter addresses the experience of public involvement in the primary care setting in the context of the potentially different roles of health authority and primary care purchasers.

Throughout the chapter, the ways in which national policy and guidance interact with local operational considerations are also examined in the context of the wider debates about governance and accountability. As we have argued, public involvement is underpinned by the continuing tension between central and local responsibilities which has dominated most major organizational reforms of the service and remains central to current debates about purchasing/providing within a primary care-led NHS. This issue is returned to at the end of this chapter but first it is important to examine the key characteristics of the wider policy and operational contexts within which public involvement is undertaken by healthcare purchasers.

## The policy context of public involvement

The White Paper *Working for Patients* (DoH 1989a) was primarily concerned with structural arrangements for the service and did not specifically address the issue of community or consumer involvement. However, one of its two objectives for action was '. . . to give patients, wherever they live in the UK, better healthcare and greater choice of the services available' (DoH 1989a: 3). In order to achieve this, the first measure presented in the White Paper was to improve the consumer sensitivity of the NHS '. . . to make the Health Service more responsive to the needs of patients, as much power and responsibility as possible will be delegated to the local level' (p. 4). The 'local level', however, did not refer to participation by local groups and individuals but rather to internal decision making within the NHS. Similarly other references to patients were in connection with organizational changes such as self-governing hospitals, GP fundholders and provider competition. There was no specific mention of the involvement of patients or local communities and, as we have seen, the limited public representation provided via local authority nomination of health authority board members was ended (Longley 1993). While the ensuing Act provided for the new district health authorities to consult widely on their purchasing plans, there was no prescription on what form this should take and GP fundholders had only to discuss their purchasing plans with health authorities. As a complex official document detailing purchasing intentions, the plan does not appear to have been the optimum vehicle for public involvement (Flynn *et al.* 1996). The concept of responsiveness did not imply the need for a direct dialogue with the public but rather a belief that this would be ensured by the market mechanisms of the consumerist approach.

Overall, therefore, the *Working for Patients* White Paper served to shift the emphasis from traditional concerns with popular democratic forms of involvement to more market-based approaches, focusing on the interaction of the individual with healthcare agencies. Its emphasis on the potential of the internal market to improve services was supported by quality targets relating to standards of service, access to services, improved information about services and an emphasis on complaints systems. Its preoccupation with extending patient choice implied that individual service users would relate to providers in the same way as did the customers of a private firm. By contrast, *Caring for People* (DoH 1989b) was very explicit about what individuals should expect from services and about the need to involve people in those services. While its focus was on community care services, there were implications for health authorities in the area of joint purchasing and provision. The White Paper placed strong emphasis on ensuring that individuals have a say in how they live their lives and over the services they need. The general themes of the document were responsiveness to individuals, choice and fostering independence. In particular, the involvement of the individual and, where appropriate their carer(s), was a consistent theme throughout the White Paper. There was also an emphasis on the role of other organizations, the need for collaboration and building partnerships in the development and delivery of services through community care planning (Wistow and Barnes 1993). In this way, *Caring for People* provided a broader view of public participation than its health service counterpart, as more user groups were defined and specific reference was made to involvement at the planning, service delivery and evaluation stages. Although its emphasis was still predominantly on information-giving and consultation, it provided an alternative model to the consumerist approach of the NHS market model.

It was the publication of *Local Voices* (NHSME 1992) which placed the issue of public involvement explicitly on the health-purchasing agenda. Its emphasis, however, was primarily on the measurement and assessment of a community's health needs and on consultation to identify key priorities for healthcare (NAHAT 1993). The document focused on the involvement of local people in purchasing decisions through '. . . a combination of information giving, dialogue, consultation and participation in decision making and feedback, rather than a one-off consultation exercise' (NAHAT 1993: 3–4). It was also acknowledged that these approaches should be dove-tailed with the efforts of providers to obtain local people's views about services. This distinction between service issues (the responsibility of the provider) and more strategic issues such as needs identification (the responsibility of the purchaser) remains central to the discussion of public involvement.

In 1994, the then Minister for Health, Dr Brian Mawhinney, argued for more public involvement in purchasing to improve the credibility and legitimacy of purchasers (NHSME 1994). Four key reasons for patient/public involvement were set out in the document:

- Health authorities need to know what local people think.
- Public consultation can help prevent local opposition to change.
- Health authorities need to establish local legitimacy for their priorities.
- Health authorities need to educate the public about health services and issues (to be responsible patients).

These arguments are interesting insofar as they reveal a range of different motives for involving the public which reflect the operational/policy and consumerist/democratic frameworks of healthcare purchasing described in earlier chapters. By so doing, they present health authorities with contrasting, and potentially conflicting, imperatives in terms of developing public involvement. The operational concern to know what local people think of current services for example has led to the involvement of the public in the process of purchasing, via activities such as health needs assessment, priority setting, consultation on purchasing plans and the monitoring of services (NHSME 1992; NAHAT 1993). These activities have taken place however within a centrally defined policy agenda which is essentially 'consumerist' in nature, promoting the rhetoric and language of the market place at the expense of that of popular democratic participation. The dominance of this agenda, with its focus on the role of the individual consumer, has encouraged local purchasers to pursue this objective via market-type mechanisms such as complaints systems and satisfaction surveys rather than by involving the wider public through representative mechanisms such as voluntary and community agencies or the CHCs.

In addition to providing a means of ensuring the quality and appropriateness of locally delivered services, the desire to know what local people think is also closely linked to the second and third criteria of preventing local opposition to change and establishing local legitimacy for service priorities. Although clearly driven by operational concerns about organizational effectiveness, these objectives may not be adequately pursued via the more individualist forms of public involvement characteristic of the consumerist approach. The process of finding out what people think of local services may require purchasers to consult with the public in its collective as well as individual forms. In doing so they may have to face the broader political questions surrounding the determination of collective needs. The identification of strategic priorities may require that the health needs of some groups of individuals are balanced against the needs of other individuals or groups and/or against those of the population as a whole. This is an issue of particular relevance to primary care purchasing (Harris 1996; Murray 1996). In addition, there are both conceptual and practical problems involved in balancing the 'needs' or 'wants' as identified by the public against those identified (or perceived) by purchasers or professionals:

> Developing effective participation will require wide consultation with the public as to their health 'wants'. What the public states as their 'wants' will not always be the same as health needs as perceived by NHS authorities. Such wants may be reasonable demands and may challenge the professional notions of need.
>
> (NAHAT 1993)

The need to resolve these issues, whilst maintaining public legitimacy for decisions taken, contrasts with the more operational imperatives driving the identification of local views. To the extent that local purchasers perceive that they are constrained by a 'democratic deficit' (Redmayne 1992) such issues may prompt them to develop a more public service-orientated approach and to search for more representative ways of involving the public (Cooper *et al.* 1995).

Finally, the concern to educate the public about health services and issues has been an increasingly important element of the central policy framework, reflected in government guidance on patient information (NHSE 1996a,c) and in government policy such as the 1996 White Paper *Delivering the Future* (DoH 1996c). This aspiration can be seen to link with operational or 'managerialist' objectives insofar as it aims to encourage a 'responsible patient' on the part of individuals and a greater understanding (ideally appreciation) by the wider public of the issues and constraints faced by purchaser organizations. In its focus on the individual relationship between the patient and the health professional, moreover, it can be seen to sit more easily with a consumerist model of involvement than a broader democratic one, prompting a 'market-research' approach to public involvement via 'lifestyle' surveys and consumer satisfaction questionnaires. There has typically been little commitment to the broader political objectives of developing patient empowerment or supporting patient action. However, while the emphasis is clearly on patient information and education, *Patient Partnership* also recognizes the wider, more strategic aims underpinning public involvement; to '. . . enable them to influence NHS service policy and planning' (NHSE 1996a: 4), echoing the general framework set out in *Local Voices* (NHSME 1992). Moreover, as we argued earlier, insofar as access to good quality information is the first step in developing a more participatory 'citizen' approach to public involvement, this objective demonstrates the potential overlap between the consumer/democratic and individualistic/collective approaches.

The policy context within which healthcare purchasers operate is therefore very complex. While it is possible in theory to distinguish between operational and policy objectives, and between consumerist and democratic approaches, is clear that the impact of these different wider frameworks is often very difficult clearly to differentiate in practice. In needs assessment and priority setting, for example, the organizational requirement to provide appropriate services for local people meshes with the broader democratic responsibilities contained within purchasers' role of 'champion of the people'. Again, practices driven by the requirements of operational accountability, such as the production of publicly accessible audited reports, can also be seen to constitute an important element of both local and central political accountability. As we have argued throughout, there is no simple policy framework surrounding the development of public involvement and the interaction of contrasting imperatives and objectives can create considerable practical problems for purchasers trying to develop appropriate approaches in local contexts. The following sections describe some of the ways in which purchasers have responded to the challenge of developing public involvement within this complex context.

## Involving the public: the experience of health authorities

In Chapter 6, purchasing was described as a staged process leading from needs assessment to evaluation. Within this process, health authorities have developed a range of methods for obtaining the views of the public. It is not our intention to examine their methods in detail as this has been done elsewhere (Sykes *et al.* 1992; Bond 1994; Bowling 1994; Hamilton-Gurney 1995; Redmayne 1995, 1996) and to do justice to such a wide and diverse range of approaches would require a book in its own right. It is important, however, to examine the processes of public involvement and the issues arising from them as they have been used by health authority and, more recently, primary care purchasers. Empirical research undertaken on public involvement clearly identifies the difficulties faced by health authority purchasers and demonstrates the convergence of consumerist and market approaches in the wider context of debates about accountability (Taylor and Lupton 1995). Research has also identified the complexities of undertaking this work within a centrally driven strategic framework (Woodward 1994; Taylor and Lupton 1995).

A main component of health authority approaches to public involvement has been the provision of information. Within purchasing organizations, this is often closely associated with a public relations or communications function (Taylor and Lupton 1995). This area of work includes the provision of information on the activities of purchasers – such as health plans, purchasing plans and annual reports – as well as information for individuals through health information services, telephone lines, individual mailings and campaigns. Circulation of purchasing plans and annual reports is a national requirement and developments beyond this, research suggests, are dependent largely on ad hoc approaches established by specific staff members rather than on any coherent information strategy. A clear national emphasis on the provision of patient information (NHSE 1996a,b; DoH 1996c), with health authorities being allocated additional resources for patient education campaigns, has driven much local activity in this area. Substantial investment has been made in consumer 'help lines' by many purchasers, through the development of local services or by contracting with specialist health information projects, which have augmented national initiatives. Health authorities typically see these developments as more than information-giving in that they also represent an opportunity to gather the views of those who call in. Such approaches are focused primarily on service users or potential users and typically encapsulate the concept of developing 'responsible patients' – those who will make less unnecessary demands on healthcare services. The aim is not necessarily to empower patients although they may be seen as a prerequisite for moving towards patient empowerment.

The use of existing groups and the provision of information in free newspapers has also been widely employed by health authorities to explain what they do and how they spend the public's money. This may be seen to reflect the search for public legitimization through greater transparency – a step towards enhancing accountability. Some health authorities have developed the information function further by organizing evening classes on the health authority role or establishing panels of people with supported access to health authority information through written material and meetings with staff (Taylor and Martin 1995). This approach mirrors the use of viewer panels in the television industry or shoppers' panels in consumer market research and aims to create an accessible supply of consumers who are better able to make informed decisions. The reasoning behind the use of such panels is that they will overcome the perceived problem of the vested or unrepresentative interests of voluntary and community groups. The issues of how representative these 'informed users' become after being provided with selected information, however, is not typically addressed.

Another reason for the use of selected panels has been the generally problematic role of public meetings. Many health authorities have experience of open health authority meetings attended by few members of the public – an experience shared by many Community Health Councils – and the perception of many health authorities is that such meetings only attract a committed public, often health professionals themselves (Taylor and Lupton 1995). The evidence from Oregon would tend to support this view (Klein 1991). Some health authorities have not seen this as a major problem as long as it is not the only method used to involve the public. For many authorities, the main experience of public meetings has been in the context of proposals to close facilities or reduce services. This has inevitably led to difficult and hostile meetings, perhaps giving an unduly negative impression of this type of involvement. One key problem of public meetings is the extent to which they have been used by health authorities to address issues which are not necessarily those of greatest concern to the public. This problem of the 'mismatch' of agendas between agencies and the public is recognized in the community involvement literature (Hallett 1987).

The problem of differing agendas is less obvious when public involvement is undertaken in relation to service reviews or areas of specific strategy development. Service review has been one of the most substantial areas of public involvement and, research suggests, potentially one of the most productive. This is in part because it enables a clear focus on the issues and on the question of who is 'the public':

> It was the area of service reviews that most health commissions could provide the most tangible examples of consumer involvement in practice. It was certainly clear that in this area of commissioning consumer involvement was easier to conceptualize and focus on for all the participants. It was usually easier to define current and potential consumers in relation to a specific service or client group and to develop a clearer agenda based on people's experience of an existing service.
>
> (Taylor and Lupton 1995: 58)

The other two central areas of public involvement identified by Taylor and Lupton (1995) as being developed by health authorities were needs assessment and service feedback. As we have seen, needs assessment was one of the key roles given to purchasers within the reformed NHS as a prerequisite for developing local purchasing/commissioning strategies, and *Local Voices* (NHSME 1992) recognized that the public should be involved in the process. Research indicates that there has been a substantial amount of health authority activity in this area, characterized by a great diversity of approach, which has raised major issues of both method and cost (Richardson *et al.* 1992; Bowling *et al.* 1992). Techniques used range from survey-based data collection, through epidemiological approaches to more public-focused and/or community-based techniques, such as participatory rapid appraisal (Cresswell 1992; Murray *et al.* 1994; Percy-Smith 1996). To an extent also, the identification of local needs and priorities has utilized the more formal procedures of joint commissioning and, through them, the contribution of community and voluntary organizations.

The diversity of approach reflects some of the complexities of defining need (Bradshaw 1972; Doyal and Gough 1991; Stevens and Gabbay 1991; NAHAT 1993) as well as the tensions of reconciling different and possibly competing needs. The fact of differences of view – between the public and the health authority and between different sections of the public – has created problems for purchasers and there are indications that it has often been used to avoid or undervalue public involvement (Flynn *et al.* 1996). Such a position is often reinforced by the perception that the interests of voluntary organizations, insofar as they are seen to be focused on a specific area of need and/or a specific group, are too vested or 'self-serving'. Yet at the same time health authorities have been actively seeking the views of individual users of health services. This interest in users may reflect the growing power and influence of the user and self-advocacy movement which intersected with the consumerist emphasis in healthcare from the mid 1980s. It may also, however, be due to the fact that it fits more comfortably with the language of the market as well as reflecting the traditional relationship between patients and medical staff.

From needs assessment, the next step in the purchasing cycle is the development of strategic plans which define what healthcare is to be purchased. Here, the evidence on public involvement becomes a little more complex. While there appears to have been substantial interest in the area of priority setting, there is little evidence of any systematic approaches being developed and the main focus has typically been on the involvement of voluntary and community group representatives in joint commissioning structures. Priority setting is one of the more developed and researched areas relating to strategic development. The approach undertaken in Oregon sparked substantial interest in the UK (Honigsbaum *et al.* 1995) and a number of health authorities attempted to involve the public in this area of activity over the years of the late 1990s (Rutt 1992a; Redmayne 1995). This remains of central policy interest given the often very public nature of debates about the rationing or 'prioritization' of service, such as the high profile 'Child B' case in 1995 (Wall 1995). As with needs assessment, health authorities have taken a range of different approaches to priority setting ranging from the 'rapid appraisal' approach (Rutt 1992a,b) to more consultative approaches (Percy-Smith 1996). Assessment of the different approaches by Bowling and colleagues (1992) concluded that a multimethod approach was potentially the best option:

A mixed methodological approach to health care prioritisation is essential. Data is needed on health needs, the evaluation of service effectiveness, local practice, and the monitoring of costs and outcomes, alongside public consultation. Hard epidemiological data reviews, combined with interviews with key people and community group members who act as representatives of the community, population surveys and booster samples appear to be the way forward.

(Bowling *et al.* 1992: 48)

Whatever the method employed, all approaches may raise similar problems in terms of how to make final decisions based on the views expressed, whilst taking into account wider public debates about healthcare priorities (Flynn *et al.* 1996; Klein *et al.* 1996).

From strategic plans, purchasers should then define their purchasing plans and there is a statutory requirement that, in doing so, they should consult widely on their purchasing intentions. As with needs identification, the method of consultation has varied between authorities (Cooper *et al.* 1995; Redmayne 1995) and there is as yet no real evidence on the value of different types of consultation process. Cooper and colleagues (1995) described the assessment undertaken by the NHS Executive in 1994 whereby 21 per cent of health authority approaches to consultation were categorized as being 'good' – but note that the definition of what constituted 'good' was not made clear. There is some evidence to support the view that consultation on purchasing intentions is somewhat tokenistic. Flynn *et al.*

(1996), for example, found that many voluntary group representatives expressed doubt about the significance of the consultation process and criticized the vague nature of the statements contained in the plans:

> 'We've had various things through the post about them (purchasing plans, etc.). But it's all totally indistinct and vague; it means nothing. They're just general statements about broad intentions; they don't actually mean anything.'
>
> (User representative, quoted in Flynn *et al.* 1996: 69)

Generally, it seems, health authorities have been highly responsive to changes in national policy in relation to public involvement and these, as we have argued, may tend to encourage some forms of involvement more than others. The *Patient's Charter* initiatives, for example, focused much attention on the achievements of specified organizational targets, possibly to the disadvantage of more community-based approaches. While, as Hogg (1995) has argued, the emphasis of the Charters on service standards may deliver some benefits for patients in terms of improving service standards (e.g. shorter waiting times or more information), they may not engage with the more substantive concerns of service users or the wider public. In particular, their engagement with a centrally driven political agenda, while giving impetus to the Charter programme, may afford: '. . . little scope for choosing local priorities with users and may be at the expense of more important standards such as those concerning the quality of care' (Hogg 1995: 18). The emphasis on organizational targets and performance measures, for example, has been accompanied by a generally low government priority accorded to more participatory initiatives such as 'Health for All'. It is not surprising, therefore, that there is little evidence of structural health authority support for longer-term, more collaborative approaches to public involvement or for community health initiatives. Although such approaches became more widespread over the mid to late 1990s, there is evidence that they were typically marginalized from mainstream purchasing activity, led and supported by enthusiastic individuals, and generally lacking in organizational support (Peckham *et al.* 1996). Apart from occasional consultation – such as on purchasing initiatives – and other very specific information-providing or giving exercises, it is not clear to what extent, if at all, such approaches have engaged with the healthcare purchasing process in a more systematic way.

Interestingly, locality approaches, often developed in collaborative projects, have provided some good examples of public involvement which have moved beyond the consumerist model and which are based on more democratic principles. However, despite the growing interest in localities within the new NHS there is little evidence of building on local collaborative models within the purchasing context. This is despite the increasing focus on the development of localities for purchasing purposes through the development of locality purchasing, multifunds, total purchasing and GP locality commissioning. From a central policy perspective, the main aim seems to have been develop the structures of primary care provision and purchasing (DoH 1996a,c; *MedEconomics* 1997). At a local health authority level the emphasis has been on generating epidemiological profiles for localities rather than on developing a more community-based focus (Peckham *et al.* 1996; Exworthy and Peckham forthcoming). It remains to be seen whether initiatives under Agenda 21 – the local authority response to the Rio de Janeiro Earth Summit on the environment – can stimulate different ways of involving the public in purchasing. Given the continued interest in local authority healthcare purchasing, it is likely that this debate is only just beginning.

## The independent voice of the consumer: the changing role of the CHCs

As explored in earlier chapters, the years of the 1990s witnessed increased public concern about the extent to which accountability within the NHS, as measured by openness of its decision-making processes, decreased following the abolition of regions and the merging of health authorities. The demise of the regional health authorities clearly removed a layer of public meetings from the NHS and there have been a number of concerns expressed about the secrecy of Trust board meetings – often justified in terms of the perceived need for commercial secrecy. Concerns over the role and accountability of board members led to an NHS review of governance in 1993 (NHSME 1993). While the review covered a wide range of issues, the final report placed great emphasis on the accountability of board members to their local communities.

The market-based assumptions underpinning the 1991 reforms led to an increased emphasis on the role of complaints as the main mechanism for ensuring accountability to individual consumers. This establishment of the Wilson Committee, which reported in 1995, recommended improved complaints procedures for providers, purchasers and general practice (DoH 1995d). While Wilson addressed a number of issues relating to complaints, the area of professional misconduct was excluded from the Committee's terms of reference. The individualist focus of the consumerist agenda, moreover, meant that, while complaint systems operated as a means of identifying problems, they provided no substantive role for the complainant beyond that afforded by the formal procedures. Nevertheless, the development of NHS complaints systems led some to argue for a decreased role for the independent Community Health Councils[1] in handling complaints, previously a central aspect of their work (Millar 1996).

The area of complaints, moreover, was not the only one in which the CHCs had to face changes over the years of the mid 1990s. The introduction of purchasing and the publication of *Local Voices* (NMSE 1992) radically altered their traditional role as the independent voice of healthcare service users (Moon and Lupton 1995). In many ways, the rhetoric of 'consumer power' on the one hand, and the reduced public accountability of health authorities on the other, would seem potentially to reinvigorate the role of the CHCs as an independent statutory mechanism for representing the interests of both 'consumers' and the wider public. An extended brief for the CHCs initially appeared to be acknowledged by government encouragement to shift from their traditional concern with monitoring service provision to a more direct focus on the purchasing function. Their involvement, moreover, would be significant: contributing '... in a major way to the evolution and monitoring of the purchasing function' (NHSME 1994: 2). At the same time, however, the realities of the developing purchasing environment served to undermine the CHCs' role in a number of central ways.

Firstly, healthcare purchasers assumed that their role as 'champions of the people' charged them with the responsibility to identify and respond to the voice of the consumer themselves (NHSME 1992), potentially supplanting the role of existing mechanisms for consumer representation (Lupton *et al.* 1995). Secondly, the existence of health authority and GP purchasers, acting as 'consumers' on behalf of local communities and 'publics', militated against the direct participation of consumers and their representatives in market transactions (Green 1990; Hudson 1992). Finally, there were explicit concerns expressed by central government about the potentially political nature of the CHCs which led to significant restraints over their role and remit in the NHS (Lupton *et al.* 1995).

As the latter discovered in their national investigation of the operation and impact of the Councils, they began increasingly to experience a central tension between their desire for independence and their need to work closely with their local health authorities. As a result the relationship of the CHCs with their local health authorities subsequent to the reforms involved a range of positions on the two central dimensions of 'opposition/collaboration' and 'independence/incorporation' (Lupton *et al.* 1995). The close and collaborative relationships of the 'HA Partners' for example contrasted with the more actively oppositional stance of the 'independent challengers'. While those working more closely with their local health authorities were not seen as having much independent input to the purchasing process, the more confrontational Councils retained greater independence, but were largely excluded from formal and informal decision-making processes. All of the Councils, however they interpreted their role, felt that the result of the reforms was to leave them very much dependent on the 'grace and favour' of their local purchasing authorities. There was a widespread view that whatever influence they did exert was largely restricted to marginal concerns such as quality assurance rather than major policy decisions about the current and future shape of the service (Lupton *et al.* 1995).

This situation was exacerbated by the abolition of the regional health authorities in 1996, which shifted the funding of the CHCs to the very agencies whose activities they were established to scrutinize. As a result of these developments, the years of the early 1990s witnessed a growing debate, not only about the role of CHCs, but also about how they should be funded and supported. Their national organization, the Association of Community Health Councils for England and Wales (ACHCEW), favoured a central funding agency, independent of the NHS structure, to regulate and support the local Councils. Proposals set out in a management consultants' review of CHCs undertaken for the Department of Health in 1996, in contrast, suggested the virtual abolition of the Councils as previously known by the removal of all their complaints work and a closer, contracted association with health authorities to work on public involvement in purchasing (Millar 1996). There were indications early in 1997 that the Department of Health had distanced itself from the recommendations of the review but, at the time of writing, the future for the CHCs remains uncertain.

## Primary care purchasing and public involvement

The definition of primary care is very complex (Gordon and Hadley 1996) and can include a wide range of NHS and non-NHS community health services as well as some hospital services such as accident and emergency. As argued in Chapter 6, the focus of primary care policy in the late 1980s and in the 1990s was on the central role of general practice as evidenced by developments such as fundholding, locality commissioning and other forms of GP-led purchasing. Traditionally, however, there has been little public involvement in UK general practice services (Heritage 1994; Peckham 1994); the central form of the public's contact with general practice has remained the doctor–patient interaction.

Little systematic empirical work has been undertaken on primary care purchasers' approaches to public involvement. What evidence there is suggests a strong reliance on traditional methods of general practice participation such as patients' participation groups (PPGs) or feedback from individual patients in their consultations with primary healthcare professionals. Some fundholders have employed more market-orientated methods such as patient surveys and the use of newsletters, suggestion boxes and even patient liaison officers. These initiatives, however, remain focused on practice populations rather than on wider communities and more sophisticated forms of engagement with public representatives and voluntary groups seem a long way off (Peckham *et al.* 1996). Even in respect of patient participation groups, as Pritchard (1994) comments, progress has been slow, with only some 3 per cent of all practices establishing such groups by the mid 1990s (although this represented over 400 groups nationwide). In addition, doubts have been expressed about who participates in such groups and the extent of their 'representativeness':

> The extent to which patient participation groups reflect the profile and needs of the practice population is unclear. It may be that the

group provides a forum for those from higher social classes in which to articulate their needs; the views of patients in social classes 3 and 4, who may be less likely to attend meetings, may therefore go unacknowledged, though their needs may be greater.

(Agass *et al.* 1991: 198)

Nevertheless, whatever their perceived limitations, the focus on patient participation groups has been substantially greater than any other developments in public participation in primary care. As discussed in Chapter 5, with the growth of community health initiatives in the 1980s, interest grew in the interactions between the broader primary healthcare team (mainly community health nursing), community organizations and the public. Although developed mainly in relation to primary healthcare provision, initiatives such as the primary care 'arts in health' movement or the establishment of community health resources in local practices (Peckham *et al.* 1996) potentially provided a basis for developing public involvement in primary care-led purchasing. However, the evidence currently suggests that these developments have not yet had much impact on the management, organization or running of general practice (Peckham 1994). With the proposals in the Labour government's White Paper, *The New NHS*, (DoH 1997b) for the development of primary care-based commissioning groups, it becomes arguably more important for general practice to involve local people, in order to maintain equity, establish local needs and priorities and determine the effectiveness and quality of healthcare services. This will require that GPs address the question of how to involve people, not only in decisions about primary healthcare services (Gillam 1992; Hastings and Rashid 1993; Harris 1996), but also in those relating to the purchasing of primary and secondary healthcare services. Undertaking the latter responsibility effectively may mean practice-based approaches combining with those being developed by health authorities and other agencies purchasing and providing health and social care.

The shift to primary care-led purchasing in this way presents many challenges for general practice. Currently it remains essentially demand driven, based on the individuals who belong to a particular practice. Adjacent practices, however, have overlapping catchment areas and patients select when and why they see their GPs. In contrast, needs assessment is based on discrete geographical areas or population subgroups and seeks to identify unmet needs as well as those which are patient-identified or otherwise known. If primary healthcare professionals, and GPs in particular, are to be drawn into wider public health debates about the equity, appropriateness and effectiveness of services, they will need to develop knowledge of local needs wider than those expressed by patients in the surgery. This approach has been effectively argued by Neeve (1994) and others. In this way, primary healthcare professionals will be drawn into the debates about public involvement with which health authorities have struggled since 1991 and which highlight the differences, and potential tensions, between the operational rationale for public involvement in terms of needs assessment or service monitoring and the broader issue of accountability to the public explicitly stated in the fundholders' *Accountability Framework* (NHSE 1995a).

## Reconciling consumerist and democratic approaches

As we suggested at the beginning of the chapter, it is impossible here to capture the range and variety of approaches to involving the public in healthcare commissioning and purchasing developed over the years of the late 1990s. Our intention has rather been to reflect some of the main approaches which have been adopted within the wider frameworks and contexts set out in earlier chapters. What is clear from the limited research on this aspect of healthcare purchasing is that there is a growing recognition, particularly within health authorities, of a potential conflict between the consumerist and democratic models of public involvement. This is often represented by a tension between a user or customer-focused approach and the broader principles of public accountability. While it has been acknowledged by both central government (NHSME 1992, 1994) and by healthcare purchasers that involving the public is an important way to ensure the accountability of both the purchasing and commissioning process, the problem has been the lack of understanding of the methods required to do so effectively. Key problems are also posed for purchasers as a result of the dichotomy, in both policy and practice, between the emphasis on consumerist approaches (consultation, complaints systems, patient surveys and patient information and education) and more democratic approaches (working with user groups, the voluntary sector and addressing issues of broader public accountability).

There is evidence that some health authorities have tried to address these tensions but, as Barnes *et al.* (1995) found in their survey of health and social service managers, while managers may appear to embrace the requirements to develop user involvement more openly than before, there is continuing scepticism about the process and a general anxiety about possible consequences that may not be easy to manage. Underlining this anxiety may be a lack of experience of public accountability on the part of managers in health authorities who have typically been confined to dealing with complaints or defending services in confrontational meetings (Taylor and Lupton 1995). In particular, there appears to be little appetite for the more open-ended types of involvement and agenda setting promoted by many user involvement organizations. This is underlined by the findings of the research in the former Wessex Regional Health Authority where managers admitted that they and their organizations had very little experience or understanding of what user or public involvement entailed (Taylor and Lupton 1995), a finding reflected by Flynn *et al.* (1996). The Wessex research also confirmed that managers remain keen to consult with 'naive' users, individual members of the public who are seen to represent no particular sectional interest, rather than with user/patient representatives, who are seen to promote particular or 'vested' interests.

One key problem that emerges from this brief review of the experience of healthcare purchasers relates to the aims and objectives of public involvement. There appears to be little clarity about the reasons why the public should be involved and this has served to heighten problems about the specific approaches to be used. This lack of clarity of purpose is perhaps not surprising given the complex context within which healthcare purchasers operate. As we have seen, the wider policy framework for public involvement is, in itself, attempting to reconcile both consumerist and broader democratic objectives, and this potential tension is overlain by complex questions surrounding the goals and nature of accountability to the public. Ultimately, it appears, much public involvement work has been shaped by purchasers striving to respond to the different and potentially competing imperatives of the wider policy context as well as those deriving from their local operational concerns. In this way the development of public involvement is drawn into the key central–local tension which Klein (1995) has identified as one of the enduring characteristics of the NHS. In particular, the emphasis on consumerist approaches at a central policy level may contrast with growing need, in the face of a perceived 'democratic deficit', for purchaser organizations to seek wider public legitimacy for their actions. The greater fragmentation that may result from the focus on primary care, however, may serve to weaken the link between health authority purchasers and 'their' publics. This may in turn mean a stronger emphasis on the consumerist model, reflecting the more individualistic nature of general practice and primary care purchasing. Against this it is clear that the broader debates about accountability and, in particular, about the role of local authorities, are unlikely to die away. These are issues to which we will return to in Chapter 9. However, before doing so, it is important to examine them in the context of the public's perspective of involvement in healthcare purchasing.

## Note

1 In Scotland, Community Health Boards have been presented with similar challenges although the funding relationship differs and the review of the CHCs in England and Wales did not relate to their Scottish counterparts.

# 8 Involvement: the response from the public

## Introduction

Interest in public involvement, both historically and currently, has tended to focus on the role of the public from an organizational or policy perspective and/or on the assessment of a particular method or approach to involvement. With the exception of those writing from within the user movement, little specific attention has been given to the ways in which members of the public themselves experience attempts to involve them in the planning or delivery of public services. This chapter will examine the issues and debates about involvement from the perspectives of those, individuals and groups, who have been involved. Given that active interest in public involvement in the NHS has until recently been sporadic, the discussion will draw more widely on evidence from public services in general.

In Chapter 4, the debates about the different types and levels of involvement and participation were discussed and this chapter will demonstrate that much of the feedback from the public on the experience of involvement is related to the particular form it takes. As we have seen, this can vary from one-off initiatives to long-term dialogue and from individual opportunities to give feedback through complaints and surveys, to the more collective experiences provided by focus groups, voluntary groups and user councils (see Figure 8.1). Chapters 5 and 6 examined the history of public involvement within the NHS, highlighting the influence of its medically dominated culture and, more recently, of the development of a market-orientated consumerism. This chapter will explore the impact of these two central features of the service on public attitudes both to involvement generally and to the specific forms it has taken.

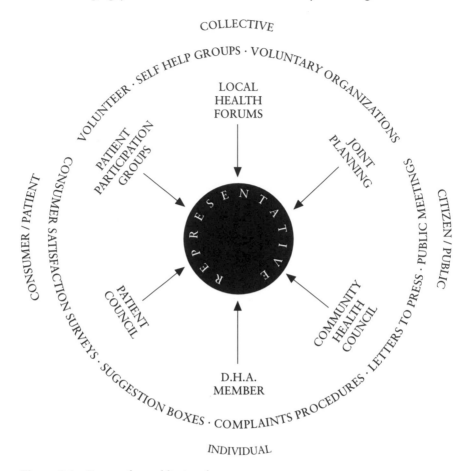

**Figure 8.1**   Routes for public involvement
*Source*: Taylor (1994)

## Who gets involved and why

The issue of who gets involved in health-related discussion and decision making, and their reasons for doing so, has been the subject of considerable debate. Suspicion of the backgrounds and motives of those willing to participate is a common reason given by managers and health professionals alike for not taking user and public involvement seriously (Taylor and Lupton 1995). Whilst there are a number of small studies which explore individuals' subjective experience of involvement, there are fewer providing information on the overall extent of public involvement, not least because of the problems of defining 'involvement'. The existing literature tends to focus on formal volunteering, examining the types of volunteers recruited by agencies such as Volunteer Bureaux and Age Concern. Such studies typically exclude the potentially large number of people involved in self-help, neighbourhood forums and other informal community activities. Figure 8.1 indicates the wide range of user involvement activities.

A review of the existing data (Davis-Smith 1992) indicates that the proportion of the public involved in some capacity is not inconsiderable. A Mori poll undertaken in 1991, for example, found that 20 per cent of the adult population had served on a committee in a voluntary capacity. Some studies suggest that those involved may not represent a cross-section of the public: certain kinds of individuals may be more likely to get involved than others and may be more likely to assume positions of responsibility. Thus the volunteer group in the Mori survey comprised a higher proportion of men than women and an earlier survey by the Charities' Aid Foundation (CAF 1987) found that 19 per cent of people serving on committees were from professional and managerial backgrounds compared with only 5 per cent from an unskilled manual background. The General Household Survey (OPCS 1987) similarly found a greater propensity for volunteers from professional backgrounds to take on formal responsibilities, such as committee work.

Other research indicates that the backgrounds of those involved may be more disparate. Thus a survey by the Patients' Association (Brotchie and Wann 1993) examined the experience of lay involvement across a wide variety of health service-related participatory mechanisms – self-help groups, Community Health Councils, advocacy schemes, community health schemes and directly in health authorities including medical ethics committees – and its findings challenge to an extent the assumptions typically made about the importance of different socio-economic backgrounds. Whilst having the necessary confidence and skills was seen to be important, many activists did not possess these characteristics at the beginning of their involvement. Progress to their current positions often owed more to the coincidence of factors such as where, why and at what level the opportunities for involvement occurred. Many individuals went through a process of personal development in order to sustain the often complex levels of involvement they ultimately held. Motivation, personal characteristics and opportunities for information, support and encouragement were all relevant to that process.

Figure 8.2 provides a model for understanding the different levels of involvement characteristic of any one community. The apex of the triangle contains those few who actively assume the roles and responsibilities of community 'representatives'. The next layer reveals a larger group prepared to get involved in starting and running specific activities close to their personal experiences/interests. The third layer represents those who may be prepared to join in relevant initiatives, but are disinclined to take an active role in running the project or group. The final layer comprises the 'non-joiners'. Feedback from users in the studies already cited indicates that involvement in the different layers of participation may vary for different individuals at different times in their lives.

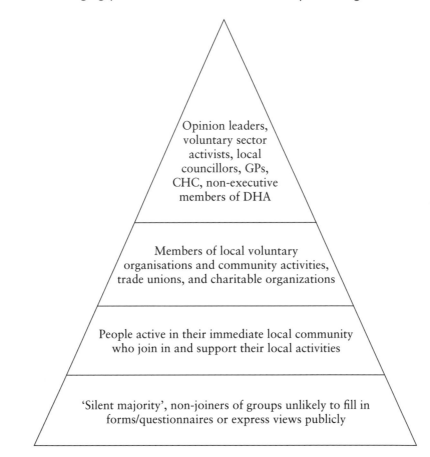

**Figure 8.2**   Levels of public involvement
*Source*: Taylor (1995: 8)

Many commentators (Leat 1977; Hatch 1983) have examined what mo-
tivates people to get and stay involved in voluntary activity. They identify
a range of reasons why people begin their involvement which may affect
the particular forms of involvement they ultimately pursue. Factors such as
gratitude for a service received, time to spare, a wish to identify with professionals and support an existing service, dissatisfaction with a service, a desire
to help others or contribute to the public good and coming from a background or community with a tradition of public service are all commonly
quoted reasons. For many, involvement begins in small ways at a level and
with a focus that is meaningful to their personal situation. As a member of
a community health project stated:

> Before I was just a local single parent struggling to deal with a large
> family by myself. I started doing things on the estate when someone

asked me to come to a tenants' meeting and this started me thinking that it was time I took some steps to stop the decline in this area and improve things for our local kids. The things just went on from there, first working with the kids and then talking to the women about family problems and health issues, now, with Jenny's help [the health visitor], working on this project and attending meetings and committees with professionals . . . it's a long way to come in six years.

(Lupton and Taylor 1997)

Piette (1990) groups individuals who get involved into two broad categories of 'defenders' and 'protesters'. The defenders are those whose primary motivation for involvement stems from a desire to support or defend a particular service; protesters are those whose involvement is triggered by a concern to express dissatisfaction or bring about change. The category to which individuals initially belong, she maintains, will affect who they mix with and the particular kind of involvement they select. Individuals' original motivation for becoming involved of course may change or evolve as a result of their experience. Defenders may grow more critical as they understand the organization better and protesters may modify their stance as they perceive the constraints surrounding the provision of the service. The evolution of individuals' motivation will be discussed further in later sections.

Much of the evidence discussed in this chapter is based on subjective accounts by people with a substantial history of involvement. This is perhaps inevitable: only a small proportion of the wider public ever becomes involved and even fewer may have the opportunity formally to reflect on their experience. A study of consumer involvement across a range of service sectors within the personal social services (Lupton and Hall 1993) however found that, even those with whom communication is seen to be difficult by professionals and researchers (elderly people, individuals with learning difficulties, children) were able (and keen) to reflect in some way on the importance of being asked their views and on the way in which it was done. This research suggests that, because people usually become involved for a specific reason – to make a complaint or to give feedback on a particular service – they are likely to focus on the ends rather than the process of involvement. Their initial evaluation of the experience will thus tend to depend on whether the desired change results (ibid.). More substantial contact may be required to establish to what extent they understood or enjoyed the experience more generally.

There is, as yet, insufficient evidence to indicate how far the new consumerist culture of the NHS has stimulated public involvement. Integral to the practical and organizational developments required to bring about a market-based healthcare system is the fundamental, but possibly much slower, process by which people begin to view themselves as consumers with an active role in managing their health and social care needs. Research on community-based health and social care services by Baldock and Ungerson (1994), for example, identified a range of ways in which individuals may

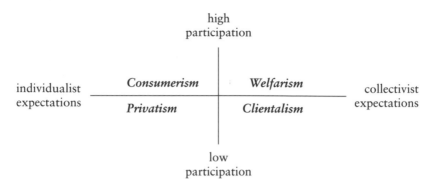

**Figure 8.3**  'Habits of the heart': models of participation in the care market
*Source*: Baldcock and Ungerson (1994: 13)

negotiate the role of service 'consumer'. Strong differences in personal pre-ferences and beliefs – the 'habits of the heart' – affect how they adjust to changes in their circumstances (Figure 8.3). The authors identified two different groups: one containing people who believed in helping themselves and being self-sufficient and the other comprising those who were commit-ted to state services and their right to access them in a time of need. Significantly each group was further broken down in relation to its mem-bers' willingness actively to ask other people for help. In the first group this involved a division between those (the 'consumerists') who were pre-pared to ask/pay for the services of neighbours, family or private care and those who prized self-sufficiency and found it difficult to request or receive help from others (the 'privatists'). In the second group this involved some being prepared to press for their rights to public services (welfarists) whilst others (the clients) were content to wait for whatever they were offered.

The way in which individuals negotiate the role of consumer is clearly relevant to their propensity to get involved. Other factors may also serve to encourage or inhibit public involvement in healthcare service provision.

## Dependency, vulnerability and the importance of identity

> From my own perspective . . . I will always be wondering what do they really think of me [when I am less well]. You think, 'Will they believe I actually need support because I'm articulate or will they really hate my guts because I upset them at a training session?'
> (Video 'Consulting for Better HealthCare', 1994,
> Forum Television)

The above quote from a mental health service user illustrates well the anxieties of many who have chosen to become involved and have been critical of the service they received. They may be concerned about being seen as a 'troublemaker' by professionals in a service vital to their survival and at a time when they are most vulnerable. This is underlined by the in-depth research undertaken by Hogg on user and patient experiences:

> The difficulties of making a complaint should not be underestimated, particularly for people who feel vulnerable and are dependent on the hospital for their ongoing care. They fear, sometimes rightly, that a complaint will be held against them.
>
> (Hogg 1995: 70)

Research indicates that some people may need considerable reassurance about the confidentiality of their views and, in some cases, may only feel able to voice opinions after their treatment is finished or they receive assurances that they can choose to go elsewhere (Taylor 1994). To the extent that choice is a reality, the consumerist agenda may in this way serve to empower some people. As we have indicated earlier, however, the possibility of 'exit' may also serve to inhibit the expression of 'voice' as people chose to leave the service rather than stay and articulate their concerns.

There are a few in depth studies (Cornwell 1984; Wilson 1993) which have examined this issue in relation to very vulnerable older people. Cornwell identifies the difference between people's private attitudes and the statements they are prepared to make in public and emphasizes the role played by low expectations and a limited sense of entitlement. Wilson describes the way direct questions are likely to elicit a public statement whilst indirect questioning may reveal more private opinions, and highlights the tendency of many older people to give researchers the answers they think they want. Thus the response of an elderly woman to a question about her experience in a hospital ward:

> They are all very nice in there and they do their best. That's the answer you want dear.
>
> (Wilson 1993: 511)

In part, this situation may reflect the fact that some elderly patients remember a time prior to the inception of the NHS when healthcare was an individual's responsibility and based on the ability to pay or charitable provision. Memories of strong national support for a collective and universal service may continue to underpin a general reluctance to be seen to criticize the quality of care. As has been discussed in Chapter 5, the contract that was negotiated for the NHS gave the public an expert-dominated and defined service, one which the politicians accepted on its behalf. There was little concern with issues of public involvement at that time (Crossman 1976); rather, the focus was on what the public could get from a service free at the point of provision. This history helps to explain the traditionally strong cultural view of the NHS as generally a 'good thing', for which individuals should be grateful and supportive. The perseverance of such an attitude is continually demonstrated in public opinion polls and emphasized by health professionals and their organizations. The past twenty years may have seen the rise of patient and consumer groups voicing some criticisms of certain aspects of the service, but overall the general support of the British public for its national health service appears to remain unshaken. Such a situation may serve to inhibit those who wish to voice an opinion, but who do not wish to appear disloyal to the service overall. This extends Hirschman's (1970) analysis of the inverse relationship between loyalty and exit by indicating that, in some cases, 'loyalty' can serve to inhibit 'voice' rather than make its expression more likely. Particularly in the context of health services, it indicates that the reluctance to complain should not be taken as the absence of concerns:

> Most people do not complain and do not want to. But this does not mean that they have nothing to say or that staff cannot learn from their experience. Complaints need to be placed firmly within quality management.
>
> (Hogg 1995: 70)

While the development of a consumerist culture with its attendant high profile for complaints and feedback may be changing people's expectations of public services (as the steep increase in complaints would appear to demonstrate), feelings of loyalty to the service and individuals' actual or perceived vulnerability in the face of powerful professionals, may serve to inhibit them from operating more actively like their counterparts in the commercial market. The issue of vulnerability may be particularly relevant in the context of primary healthcare, where the role of the 'family doctor' as gatekeeper to community and hospital-based services is crucial.

The discussion in earlier chapters of the distinctions between the consumerist and democratic approaches have highlighted the very different ways in which they describe the relationship between those who provide services and those who receive them. Burns *et al.* (1993) has attempted to provide a framework for understanding these differences:

> Consumer describes the relationship of a person to a product... Customer describes a relationship of a person receiving a service to an organization offering services ... Client describes a relationship of a person receiving a service to another person offering services ... Citizen describes the relationship of a person to the state.
>
> (Burns *et al.* 1993: 40)

Burns's framework, however, is relatively neutral in terms of the power relations underpinning these different roles. Yet, as Beresford and Croft (1993: 84) have argued, the use of language is inextricably linked to the issue of power: 'Language raises many issues for involvement. Central is its relation with power. Language is not neutral. Labels like "the old", "the unemployed", "the mentally ill" are imposed upon people.' Some service users have, as a result, resisted attempts to recast them in the market-based roles of 'customers' or 'consumers' and selected instead terms such as 'survivors' or 'users' which they feel more accurately describe their situation. Organizations such as Survivors Speak Out for mental health service users and People First, representing people with a learning difficulty, illustrate this well. Taylor (1993) argues that terms such as 'user,' 'survivor', 'subject', 'recipient', are more appropriate insofar as they highlight the power imbalance inherent in services where access is mediated by professionals and/or managers. Use is not always voluntary and choice can be limited or non-existent. The traditional relationship of doctor and patient, for example, is based on a fundamental imbalance of power. The role of the patient is an essentially passive one; the patient is dependent on the doctor not only to define the service received, but also to decide whether there is access to any service at all. In traditional medical thinking, patients enter into contracts with their doctors which allow their bodies to be seen as the practitioner's 'work objects' (Stacey 1976: 176). Williamson (1992) notes that much of the debate between individual patients, their organizations and medical professionals is focused around these expectations and the extent to which they conflict with a more holistic approach to patient care which emphasizes the patient's autonomy, the link between physical and emotional health and the wider social context of the patient. Such debates are captured clearly in the contrasts between the medical and social models of disability (Oliver 1990). Here the issues tend to be more pressing for those who, as a result of a need for ongoing care, may find their identity and overall quality of life greatly affected by interventions which concentrate solely on their medical condition.

It could be argued that the consumerist approach to doctor–patient relationships addresses some of these issues, insofar as it emphasizes the importance of consumer power and patient involvement in decision making. Against this, however, it can be argued that its narrow focus on particular services makes it less likely that wider social issues are addressed, such as the ability of people with disabilities to live as full members of the community with access to an income and employment. It is precisely these kind of issues which have led user organizations to press for greater democratic involvement in the political process in addition to specific involvement at the level of service delivery, and to view the two dimensions as integral to each other. Many commentators writing from the perspectives of users, consumers or the public argue that the consumerist approach, with its emphasis on the individual, ignores and diminishes the contribution of those user groups which are built on the principles of collective action. Perhaps not surprisingly, therefore, the apparent recognition of the patient perspective in the development of *The Patient's Charter* standards (DoH 1991) appears typically to have been accompanied by a growing distrust of the input from user organizations and voluntary organizations, which are seen to represent narrow sectional interests.

> Some corporate rationalisers seem to think there is a population of naive consumers who subscribe to neither professional nor consumerist standards, but to a third authentic set, if only what that is could be discovered.
>
> (Williamson 1992: 40)

**Table 8.1**   Purchasers' perspectives on the public's role

| Type | Possible characteristics | Likely contribution to the service |
|---|---|---|
| Naive user | Jo public/person on the street<br>Focus on own experience<br>Opinions not informed by professional knowledge<br>Anecdotal experience | Answers questionnaires and surveys<br>Recruited to focus groups/users helpline |
| Professional user | Involved in several aspects of healthcare<br>'Gratitude factor'<br>May identify with professional staff and their interests<br>Too close to providers<br>Health service enthusiast | Fund-raising<br>Volunteering<br>League of Friends<br>Available for committees, planning groups, events |
| Vested interest user | May have long experience of healthcare<br>Long-term user<br>Some particularly bad experience<br>Axe to grind<br>Commitment to change or to improve a particular aspect of the service | Campaigning and lobbying<br>Letters to press and media<br>Frequent contact with service<br>Uses public meetings, consultations, etc. to raise relevant issues<br>Alternative research to make case for change |
| Informed user | Active in a range of community activities and strong links<br>Sense of public service/duty<br>Other responsibilities allow flexibility<br>Interest, enthusiasm and confidence<br>Proactive in becoming informed | Acts as representative on planning and project groups<br>Gets involved in a range of activities in the service<br>Invited to contribute to conferences, workshops, training events, etc. |

*Source*: Taylor and Lupton (1995: 24).

The desire of managers to keep control the involvement agenda, and the concern of professionals to retain power over the services they provide, may combine to produce a powerful barrier to the involvement of the public in healthcare decision taking. In their study of public involvement in health authorities, Taylor and Lupton (1995) found that purchasers tended to divide those who got involved into four categories (Table 8.1). As already indicated, the 'naive user' was typically viewed as the 'real' or authentic user whose unbiased views were particularly valued and sought out by managers. Many public involvement initiatives have been targeted at this group, typically with the intention of educating individuals in the role of 'responsible patient' (Taylor and Martin 1995).

'Professionalized users' were those seen to have long-standing relation-ships with health professionals and were viewed suspiciously as only voic-ing the opinions and interests of the health providers on which they were dependent: Piette's NHS 'defenders'. The 'vested interest users' were seen to be more independent and critical, but constrained by the limited per-spectives of the particular group or interest they represented. 'Active users' were those lay people who had been able to establish credibility for their perspective, and a more general recognition of their 'case' or cause, as a result of their personal skills and/or by developing allies within the organ-ization. It is, of course, difficult to maintain a clear distinction between these two latter groups; in practice the difference between them tends to lie in the eye of the beholder. Consumers themselves were aware of being given different labels depending on the attitude and level of understanding of the person so doing. Some reported that were described by all these labels by different managers and health professionals within the same organization, often within a single encounter (McGrath and Grant 1991). For many, the concern to establish and maintain credibility as a legitimate 'voice' of the consumer in the face of such shifting evaluations of their role, was a constant source of anxiety.

The power of professionals, especially in the health service, may make it particularly difficult for the involved public openly to maintain a strong independent view. Willamson's (1992) study of consumer action in the NHS highlights the importance of consumer and user groups gaining the sup-port of key professionals as allies and advocates. The strength of the alliance between users and professional may go some way to explaining the resist-ance of many health purchasers to the 'professionalized user' (Taylor and Lupton 1995). People who become involved in a complex arena such as the NHS may benefit greatly from the guidance of those inside the service in order to make an impact, especially when they have poor access to indep-endent advice and support. Those, such as groups within the user movement, who can draw upon independent help, in turn may have to work hard to gain access to health service decision-makers, possibly making compromises between their independence and the more direct opportunities for influence in so doing (Lindow 1993; Williamson 1992; Lupton *et al.* 1995). It should be remembered that the user groups currently enjoying recognition within the health service have been operating for many years, largely unacknow-ledged within the NHS.

In contrast, many examples of public involvement in the NHS, such as volunteering and fund-raising activities, are essentially supportive and un-critical of the service. This has been the traditional role for the lay person within the NHS, complementing that of the individual patient, and fully endorsed by both managers and professionals. Richardson *et al.* (1992) in their study of patient participation groups (PPGs), for example, illustrates the extent to which the groups function as a source of apparently uncritical support for the practice in question. Her study strongly confirms and illuminates the concept of the 'professionalized user'. Lupton and Taylor's (1997) examination of PPGs as part of a wider project looking at participation at the primary care level, identified the difficulties experienced by those participating in developing a strong independent voice and in expressing opinions which contradict those of the doctors in their practice. The groups studied were perceived to be struggling with their primary purpose: whether it was to help the doctors to represent themselves more effectively to their patients or to assist the patients to represent themselves better to the doctors. Some groups were attempting to fulfil both roles with some difficulty, but others appeared to find it easier to adopt the practice support, volunteering and fund-raising model described by Richardson *et al.* (1992). Discussions with PPG members revealed a range of reasons for this stance, including the close dependence of the groups on GPs for information and guidance, problems for a group that has not been mandated by the wider patient group and anxieties about people criticizing or upsetting the key professionals responsible for their access to healthcare.

Even where GPs were interested in developing greater public participation in practice decision making, research suggests they lacked the knowledge of what involvement processes entailed, the skills to facilitate their development and/or had limited access to appropriate support (Lupton and Taylor 1997). In contrast, the same research looked at examples of community health projects which had been funded and developed outside the NHS through voluntary grant aid or 'Healthy City' initiatives. People in these projects had strong and well-developed views about their communities' health needs and their experience of current services. Typically, however, this did not involve direct contact with local health professionals by whom, those in the projects maintained, their input was neither understood nor welcomed.

One of the effects of the more consumerist climate within the NHS in the 1990s has been to force consumer and user groups to justify their claims to speak on behalf of consumers as well as to develop new roles in the involvement process. Increasingly these groups have been encouraged to act as advisors to public bodies planning or undertaking consultation, helping them to understand how best to access the wider views of the public. Interestingly, some of these groups have been accorded a shift in status from 'vested' public to 'active users' as purchasers begin to appreciate the complexities of accessing the 'naive' consumer within tight budgetary constraints. Lindow (1993) identifies four roles for the active user: representing their own direct experience; offering a user perspective; acting as an advisor in a consultation or training process; or representing an identified group or constituency to whom they are directly accountable. Too often, he argues, lay people working in a voluntary capacity are expected to take on the extra task of being involved in health authority initiatives, as well as taking personal responsibility for sustaining their links with the people they are supposed to represent. Certainly the organized user movement has learned painful lessons from involvement in activities such as joint planning. These included the perception that individual representatives had been coopted into statutory organizations, disillusionment over the lack of significant progress and concern about the tokenistic nature of user participation (McGrath 1989). The energies of many, particularly those suffering from long-term illnesses or disabilities, have been exhausted by the often stressful and long drawn out encounters with health authority personnel unused to dealing appropriately with user representatives. Many have found they are held responsible, by those they are seen to represent, for the decisions reached by the committees they join. As a result, some have assumed the independent role of paid consultants rather than user 'representative' to avoid being held personally responsible by other users for unpopular decisions.

Comprehensive research into the general public's view of representation has yet to be undertaken in this country. A survey carried out in Canada (Abelson *et al.* 1995) explored the issue with a range of different groups of citizens. They asked first how people felt about involvement as individuals and second how far they perceived that groups with similar characteristics could be seen to represent the wider population. There were marked differences in the responses of different groups, reflecting their varying sense of how society perceived the status of their particular group. In all groups, however, a distinction was drawn between individuals' belief that they personally had something to offer to consultation and involvement and their perception of the validity of their group acting in a representative capacity. Similarly, those consulted by Lupton and Hall (1993) drew a clear distinction between their willingness to comment on their personal experience of a particular service and their ill-preparedness to speak on behalf of others using the same service.

## Good practice from the public perspective

There have been many attempts to reflect on the issues raised above and to produce guidelines to assist health authorities to develop public involvement more effectively. Hogg (1995) makes the point that *The Patient's Charter* (DoH 1991), whilst being the first produced by the NHS itself, was preceded by a range of charters and guidelines for good practice produced by many different consumer, user and voluntary organizations. The *Charter for Children in Hospital* was produced by the National Association for the Welfare of Children in Hospital (now known as Action for Sick Children) in 1984 (NAWCH 1984), the Association of Community Health Councils developed its *Patient's Charter* in 1986 (ACHCEW 1986), followed by the *Charter for Carers* from the Carers' Alliance in 1989 and the *Charter for People in Pain* (SHIP 1992) produced by the organization Self Help in Pain. These national efforts were often mirrored by efforts at a local level, one example being the *Code of Good Practice on Consultation* produced by the Wiltshire Development Forum (WDF 1992).These documents were all designed to raise awareness of the user perspective in relation to different aspects of health service provision and have been used as a basis for negotiating more effective local user-based partnerships and practical changes. The NAWCH charter, for example, has been adopted by hospital trusts throughout the country and the Carers' Alliance charter has resulted in many locally based initiatives. The Wiltshire *Code of Good Practice on Consultation* was formally adopted both by the Wiltshire Health Authority and the local social services department.

Whilst she concedes that the Government's *The Patient's Charter* is part of a growing trend to give greater recognition to the concerns of patients, Hogg (1995) contrasts the market-consumer basis of the *Charter* with the citizen-rights approach of those developed by user groups. Whereas *The Patient's Charter* concentrates on specific procedural issues in acute care, the user-based charters emphasize more holistic aspects of illness, the social–healthcare interface and the wider rights of citizenship and personal autonomy. Hogg also argues that the rigidity and speed of implementation of *The Patient's Charter* gave little scope for managers to negotiate local priorities, a key feature of the earlier user charters, and so risked compromising the positive aspects of a national charter by it being seen by local users as being no more than a political public relations exercise.

Further evidence on user perspectives on good practice is provided by a three-year action research project on public involvement carried out in one health authority by Taylor and Martin (1995). Working closely with health authority personnel, a variety of user and voluntary groups and a range of individual users through involvement initiatives, the project identified many different levels at which good practice needed to be developed. In the first place, it demonstrated the importance of the organization as a whole examining how far it created an impression of openness and a desire for feedback from its users. This was in accordance with the wider operational requirements of Total Quality Management and included such issues as the accessibility of services, responsiveness to comments and complaints and provision of a range of opportunities for dialogue at both formal and informal levels. The need to ensure that those staff in first contact with service users or the public understood and supported user involvement was also demonstrated. The project found that, however well consultation events were organized, it was crucial that they had the backing and support of grass-roots staff. This was because service users tended to seek reassurance and additional information from those health service professionals they knew and trusted. If these professionals did not know about the initiative, or perceived it negatively, it could serve to discourage the involvement of individual service users, unless alternative support and validation was provided by, for example, a self-help group or voluntary organization.

A second level of good practice, based on the first, related to the quality of information on the objectives of the organization, how it worked and the services it offered. The way in which information was provided, as well as its content, was found to be important. Factors such as ensuring a range of formats, taking account of different levels of knowledge and understanding, being non-judgmental and accurate and giving attention to the language used (particularly avoiding jargon) were all identified as important by members of the public who got involved. The importance of providing opportunities for people to discuss and seek further explanation/clarification of the information they received was also stressed. Mechanisms for improving the quality of information included the availability of front-line staff, the provision of an identifiable member of staff or information service and reference to other relevant organizations such as CHCs, voluntary and self-help organizations.

A final area identified as requiring attention was the organization's practice in relation to equal opportunities. This included not only the existence of a written policy, but concrete evidence of its implementation as demonstrated by the physical accessibility of all aspects of its services, cultural sensitivity, attention to the communication and language needs of different groups and awareness of the negative effects of all types of stereotyping. Equal opportunity issues were seen to be particularly sensitive in consultation and feedback events in terms of the organization overtly recognizing the efforts made by people to be involved and being prepared to give attention to issues such as the timing and location of events, the care of dependants and the provision of transport and expenses when necessary. Finally, an understanding of the place of advocacy support was identified as being vital for a much wider range of people than was typically perceived by health authorities (Lupton and Taylor 1997).

The survey by the Patients' Association (Brotchie and Wann 1993), mentioned earlier, provided a more specific focus to good practice by identifying a clear requirement for training on involvement, not only for the public, but also for health authority staff to improve their ability to work with lay people and to understand the nature and value of their input. The report highlights the importance of communication between the patients and professionals/managers in overcoming the differences between the perceived 'objective' and generalized expert view grounded in scientific knowledge and the subjective, particularistic view based on the actual experience of lay representatives. There is a place for both perspectives and their relative strengths and weaknesses need to be understood and respected by all parties in any consultation process. The survey by the Patients' Association (Brotchie and Wann 1993) highlighted the concerns felt by many lay representatives that their perspective was not valued. Some reported that their input was overshadowed by the predominance of the expert perspective. Others felt confused and mystified at the way things were discussed, and ultimately silenced by, the majority. Still others were angry because they felt they represented a token presence, whose views were patronized and devalued by other participants. Experiences such as these make understandable the demand by some user and lay representatives to attend committees and consultation events in sufficient numbers to even out the balance. The Patients' Association makes the case for more joint training to take place between lay representatives and professionals to ensure that they are able to participate on more equal terms.

The report also highlights the need for health authorities to clarify their responsibilities for the way feedback is given to the wider population. This entails being well enough informed about the make up of the relevant constituency and being realistic about how far those acting as representatives can actually fulfil their function. Health authorities, it is argued, need to be clear about the importance of networking within their communities as well as about the different methods required to ensure representation of groups who do not have a strong local voice. Many lay representatives can draw on their own development process from 'naïve' to 'active' user to act effectively as advisors on further local development work. It is important that responsibility for feedback is given a higher profile in all areas of public involvement, in order to benefit the many lay representatives with no organized user group to support them. Particularly where people are being expected to fulfil some kind of representational role, they will require resources to do the job properly. This should include adequate time and resources to undertake consultation and documentation that is written in accessible language and formats. Health authorities are used to their own systems and timescales and can be slow to understand or take into account the constraints on outside organizations, which often rely on volunteer help and exist for reasons other than simply responding to official consultation documents. Brotchie and Wann (1993) make the point, echoed by many other commentators (NCVO 1981; Wistow 1992), that the voluntary sector infrastructure which has traditionally provided the necessary training, support and coordination for links with statutory agencies, is increasingly under strain or, in many places, is virtually non-existent. Consideration should be given to the question of whether those organizations responsible for making decisions about public services should bear the responsibility for providing the training and information necessary for members of the public effectively to take part in consultation initiatives.

We have described how the new consumerist culture of the NHS has increasingly placed the responsibility on managers to make direct links with their populations of user/potential user populations. In order to discharge this responsibility, those managers need to possess the necessary skills and resources as well as the knowledge and understanding of how to do so effectively. The approach to involvement based on the consumerist model however may, insofar as it tends to concentrate on individualized contact and on the limited types of feedback discussed in Chapter 4, inhibit the development of knowledge and experience of more collective forms of involvement. Such a situation may be worsened by the movement to a primary care-led NHS. As we have seen, what little research evidence there is (Wistow and Barnes 1993; Pritchard 1994; Peckham *et al.* 1996) indicates that, with a few significant exceptions, awareness of the infrastructure needed to support effective public involvement, is virtually non-existent at the level of primary care.

The evidence discussed in this chapter indicates that consumer and public representatives commonly experience difficulties as a result of power imbalances and tokenism in their contacts with public services. They stress the need for independent sources of support and advocacy to help lay representatives develop the confidence to voice their views. In some areas of involvement, such as within the user movement, this need has been articulated, but research suggests that it may be just as important, if less well expressed, in all areas of public involvement. Its absence is reflected in the reluctance of individuals to give honest feedback or to believe that their input is really welcomed. It is expressed in the concerns of those people who take part in user panels and focus group discussions about whether their individual views are taken to represent those of the wider public. As independent voluntary organizations are encouraged to compete for funding with statutory providers in the new 'mixed economy' of health and social care services, they may increasingly be required to take on aspects of a service culture which could compromise their ability to provide the credible, independent base for advocacy and support needed for effective involvement.

# 9 The future of public involvement

## Introduction

Throughout this book we have argued that there is a specific framework within which public involvement takes place which is characterized by the consumerist/democratic and operational/policy dichotomies set out in Chapters 2, 3 and 4. In Chapter 7 we described the ways in which this wider framework gives rise to different and possibly contradictory imperatives surrounding the development of purchasing. We have also argued that this framework is not peculiar to health but relates to wider changes in the management and organization of public services that occurred during the 1980s. As described in Chapters 2 and 3, these changes raise important questions about local governance and political accountability, and the introduction of the NHS internal market in 1991 heightened their relevance to the purchasing and provision of healthcare services. However, as we have argued in Chapter 5, this framework has also been shaped by the historical development of public involvement in health and by the enduring tension between central and local responsibilities and between managerial and professional power. The aim of this book has been to examine the ways in which health authority purchasers are attempting to make sense of this framework for public involvement in developing their responsibilities as 'champions of the people'.

While the reforms of 1991 established the broad organizational context for the NHS internal market, the shape of the service has continued to evolve with the increasing decentralization of healthcare provision and purchasing to the primary care level. At the same time there has been a centralisation of NHS structures with the abolition of regional health authorities, the creation of regional offices of the NHS Executive and the reduction in the number of health authorities through the merger of the former DHAs and FHSAs. In such circumstances it is becoming more difficult to prescribe roles and responsibilities in relation to public involvement given that, alongside these structural developments, the functions of regions, health authorities and primary care have also continued to evolve over time. The Primary Care Act 1997 and the Labour government's proposals for *The New NHS* (DoH 1997b) will bring further key changes to the operation of health authority and general practice/primary care purchasers. As the former move towards performance management roles with diminishing responsibilities for direct purchasing, the latter will assume the major purchasing role with development of Primary Care Groups and Trusts.

In this concluding chapter, we will review the key policy frameworks shaping public involvement in the late 1990s, draw out key lessons for managing public involvement in both health authorities and primary care and identify the central issues for developing public involvement in healthcare purchasing. We will also return to the broader debate about the relationship between consumerist and democratic approaches to public involvement and how these relate to more general questions about the nature and function of health and other public sector services.

## The impact of national policy and guidelines

Over the years since the introduction of the internal market, there has been a distinctive shift of emphasis in central policy and guidelines relating to public involvement. While the dominant themes have remained broadly consumerist in nature, the publication of *Local Voices* (NHSME 1992) and the emphasis on accountability in guidance on governance have appeared to support a broader, more democratic approach to public involvement. The focus on the role of the individual patient, rather than on the more collective forms of 'the public', however, has been an enduring feature of central policy statements. In recent years, this has been reflected by a growing emphasis on patient information and education (NHSE 1996a; DoH 1996c) and the development of the idea of the 'responsible patient' who makes wise choices about his/her lifestyle and who uses health services appropriately. In this conceptualization, the public, or more explicitly the patient, is seen as acting as the informed consumer of healthcare, weighing up the costs and benefits of alternative strategies of care and treatment. This notion of individual responsibility and the individualistic emphasis of public health and health promotion advocated in government policy in the early 1990s (DoH 1992b), can be seen to sit comfortably alongside the market rhetoric and more managerialist focus characterizing the NHS in the early and mid-1990s.

The increased attention given to patient involvement since the mid 1980s has not been confined to the purchasing of healthcare services. Involvement in the provision of healthcare services has also been a central issue, reflected in the work undertaken by the King's Fund in its 'Promoting

Patient Choice' programme (see, for example, Hope 1996). Even more than in the purchasing context, however, the debates about involvement in service provision have focused on the individual role of 'the patient'. This national policy guidance, through the *NHS Planning Priorities and Guidance* as well as through documents such as *Patient Partnership* (NHSE 1996a) places clear responsibilities on health authorities in terms of informing and responding to the views of patients. The individualistic basis of public involvement underpins the responsibilities of both purchasers and providers, moreover, not only in respect of promoting '. . . user involvement in their own care . . .' and '. . . making services more responsive to the needs and preferences of users' but also in respect of more strategic decision making by '. . . ensuring that users have the knowledge, skills and support to enable them to influence NHS service policy and planning (NHSE 1996a: 4).

These latter objectives comprise the overall *Patient Partnership* strategy to be taken forward at a national level by the NHS Executive but also to be delivered at a local level through 'concrete action for patients' (p. 4). Interest in the needs and views of the individual patient/user has also been developed at the professional or practitioner level. Thus a report by the Royal Pharmaceutical Society (RPSGB 1997) recognized the importance of bringing a patient perspective to the decisions about medicine-taking, in the interests of both efficacy and cost effectiveness. The focus on the individual is also evident in debates about clinical effectiveness, with patient involvement being a key element of the NHSE's approach to this issue (NHSE 1996b) and recognized as essential in developing evidence-based patient choice (Hope 1996). Recent years have seen the emergence of a number of consumer health information services (Gann and Buckland 1996) and, from April 1997, the establishment of a national project on evidence-based consumer information at the Help for Health Trust based in Winchester, Hampshire.

While central policy and guidance on public involvement has thus placed a strong emphasis on patient involvement, it has not been the only force shaping the development of this area of purchasing activity. The restructuring of the NHS, through the reorganization of regions and health authorities (1995 Health Authorities Act) and the promotion of a primary care-led NHS (NHSE 1994, 1996c; DoH 1996a,c, 1997), has also had a significant impact on the context and characteristics of public involvement. In particular, the process of organizational change has had major implications for the operational and strategic roles of both health authority and primary care purchasers. There is little evidence as yet on the way in which these different roles have played out in practice. Studies of fundholding by the Audit Commission (1996) and early data from the Total Purchasing Projects evaluation (Total Purchasing National Evaluation Team 1997), however, suggest that general practice purchasers have mainly addressed operational purchasing tasks and that few have managed successfully to grasp a more strategic purchasing role. The delineation of roles between different purchasing organizations was more clearly mapped out by the incoming Labour government in 1997 (DoH 1997b).

As argued in Chapter 7, although there has been no official support for a local authority role in healthcare on the part of any of the main political parties over the 1990s, the possibility has remained of interest to local authorities keen to emphasize their democratic credentials (Cooper *et al.* 1995; Harrison 1997). The Green Paper on mental health services (DoH 1997a) published in early 1997, proposed alternative structural arrangements for services designed to bring health and local authorities together in new agency forms. Despite this, the debate about purchasing roles remains predominantly health service focused, involving the local authorities only through the collaborative arrangements of Agenda 21 Committees or 'Health for All'/'Healthy City' initiatives – themselves possibly on the wane. It is possible, however, that the changing role of health authorities and the decentralization of purchasing may reactivate this debate. Increasingly, local authorities are themselves become purchasing agencies with less responsibility for direct provision and may, as a result, be seen to be well placed to contribute to a strategic healthcare purchasing role (Cooper *et al.* 1995; Hudson 1997). Debates about inequalities in health (DoH 1995a) increasingly recognize the important contribution of local authority services (Kawachi and Kennedy 1997) and it is clear that, despite the limitations of electoral representation, local authorities provide a broader democratic base than healthcare purchasers and may, as a result, command greater public legitimacy. Currently, however, the question of local authority involvement in the healthcare agenda remains largely unresolved and lacks government support (DoH 1997b, 1998).

## The role of health authorities

As the main purchasers of both primary and secondary healthcare services, health authorities have developed a variety of approaches to public involvement over the years of the 1990s. They are doing so, as we have seen, in a context of continual organizational flux. The development of fundholding and locality commissioning, shifting purchasing away from central health authority organizations towards primary care and localities has been of key significance. These changes have raised fundamental questions about the role of health authority purchasers more generally, not just in relation to public involvement. It is clear, however, from the experiences of the total purchasing sites (Total Purchasing National Evaluation Team 1997) that health authorities will continue to play a major role in strategic purchasing – particularly in relation to the provision of public health services in the areas of needs assessment and priority setting – but that this may be more of a regulatory role, shaping the overall framework and mediating between purchasers and providers (DoH 1997b, 1998). In discussions with senior health authority managers the term 'market regulator' has been used to describe this new role (Exworthy and Peckham forthcoming).

In relation to public involvement, health authorities may adopt a similar role in terms of defining and supporting the overall framework. It has long been recognized that, in order to develop and sustain community involvement – whether in terms of user and voluntary group involvement or wider public involvement – there is a need for some form of infrastructure (DoH/KPMG 1992; McGrath and Grant 1992; Wistow 1992). The health authority role, for example, will involve supporting joint planning and commissioning arrangements in partnership with local authorities. Although these arrangements will need to be realigned following local government boundary reform and the move towards localities (Exworthy and Peckham forthcoming), such a move could strengthen agency involvement at a primary care level. As health authorities begin to develop a more strategic purchasing role in the future, they will need to engage in public involvement activities which cut across locality or primary care purchasing arrangements. Key roles for health authorities in the future may, therefore, be to support public involvement in the following ways:

- through direct involvement with the public;
- by providing local mechanisms for involvement – supporting the infrastructure – including establishing and/or supporting mechanisms such as joint commissioning structures and locality forums, or providing specialist expertise in methodology;
- by monitoring the activity of primary care purchasers to ensure that public involvement has been undertaken;
- by acting as a market coordinator of primary care purchasers and providers.

In these ways, health authorities would stimulate and regulate the activities of purchasers in their area and, thereby, ensure that the views of the public were elicited. To do so, they will clearly need to develop effective managerial mechanisms for achieving these goals within the restricted resources available. They will also need to engage explicitly with the requirements of national policy guidelines such as *Local Voices* (NHSME 1992), the *Accountability Framework* (NHSE 1995a) and *Patient Partnership* (NHSE 1996a). This will require addressing both the consumerist/individualistic and democratic/collective contexts of public involvement. Undoubtedly, primary care purchasers will look to health authorities for specialist and contextual support as they will be facing strict resource limitations – both in terms of skills and staff. The development of specialist roles on the part of health authorities will therefore become important and, although their public involvement activity has hitherto been limited, the evidence of previous chapters suggests that they may now possess considerable accumulated experience to pass on to primary care purchasers.

## The role of primary care purchasers

Primary care purchasers will be the cornerstone of healthcare purchasing as the NHS moves into the twenty-first century (DoH 1997b, 1998). To bring primary care purchasers up to the level of public involvement activity of even the least progressive health authorities will require a substantial culture change within general practice as the key driver of primary care. As we have argued in earlier chapters, the public involvement agenda of primary care purchasers is shaped by the operational dimensions of the purchasing role and by requirements in respect of accountability as set out in the *Accountability Framework* (NHSE 1995a). However, as we have also discussed, historically general practice has not significantly been engaged in public involvement activity (Peckham 1994; Peckham *et al.* 1996) and is itself typically used as a proxy for the public's views (Rutt 1992a; Klein *et al.* 1996). In its study of fundholding, the Audit Commission (1996) found a poor record of involving the public, even among the 'first-wave' fundholders. While the length of time involved in purchasing was clearly a salient factor in whether practices had engaged with the public involvement agenda, more important was the development of the organization to a point where it was able to address more strategic purchasing goals. The Audit Commission found this to have been achieved by only a few of the practices surveyed. Fundholders had, in the main, undertaken predominantly operational purchasing tasks with an emphasis on contracting. Such an approach has not generally required the focus on areas such as needs assessment and service development which may carry more of an imperative to involve the public.

While the emphasis on operational rather than strategic concerns undoubtedly provides some explanation for the lack of public involvement in primary care purchasing, it has also been affected by two other factors. The first is the extent to which a primary care-led NHS, epitomized by general practice, is able to address public involvement in purchasing, given its traditional focus on service provision. The very nature of general practice as independent contractors working with individual patients suggests that there may be a reluctance to share decision making with other organizations and people. The second, related, issue is whether the new primary care purchasers will have the organizational and management capacity necessary to pursue this area of work. Undertaking public involvement effectively takes time and resources. Even with considerable personal and organizational support, there is no guarantee that primary care organizations will have the capacity or inclination for public involvement. In small organizations, staff already carry heavy caseloads and finding additional time can be difficult. Also, there is little management capacity in primary care and the development of purchasing is, in itself, a complex management task requiring the development of many new skills. Evidence suggests that, while a few practices have well-developed approaches to involvement and some have the basis for moving forward via initiatives such as patient forums, newsletters and surveys (Peckham *et al.* 1996), the majority of practices will need help to address this area of activity. In some practices the role of the patient participation group has developed to discussing more strategic issues. In the Wessex research, for example, some GPs referred to the potential of these groups to operate like school parent governors or the lay members of health boards (Lupton and Taylor 1997). However, even a cursory reading of the literature on primary care purchasing demonstrates that there is little interest in the area of public involvement (Glennerster *et al.* 1994; Audit Commission 1996; Smith *et al.* 1996; Williams 1996). Without a clear understanding of public involvement, and the advantages it can bring to the organization and its population, its development may be considered a minor organizational objective, the *Accountability Framework* notwithstanding.

Since the early 1990s there has been a tendency for general practices to form collaborative arrangements, either formally (through multifunds, GP commissioning groups, total purchasers) or informally (through locality arrangements). These approaches have been actively encouraged by government (DoH 1996a,c) whose policy now favours the formation of locality led commissioning (Smith *et al.* 1996). Some argue that, in this way, general practice will be able to target purchasing on a population rather than a practice-list basis and thus adopt a more strategic approach. It is also, perhaps, at this level that primary care may be able to engage more effectively in public involvement by pooling resources, engaging in joint commissioning structures and working collaboratively with local statutory and voluntary agencies. Nevertheless, it is clear that the broader potential of primary care-based purchasing may be limited by the need to manage tensions between provision and purchasing – particularly at practice level – in the context of restricted resources. This suggests that primary care and health authority purchasers may need to form alliances for the development of aspects of purchasing activity such as public involvement.

## Managing public involvement

Despite the proliferation of reports and documents addressing the question of public involvement (Sykes *et al.* 1992; Cooper *et al.* 1995; Hamilton-Gurney 1995; Taylor and Lupton 1995), health authorities and their managers continue to identify the key problem as being 'how to do public involvement'. Concerns are expressed, for example, about the relative merits of different methods of involvement and/or about how 'representative' or 'vested' are the views of those who get involved. Many of the difficulties experienced, however, such as how public involvement fits into other areas of purchasing activity and how to balance the views of the public against other inputs such as clinical perspectives and national policy/guidance, arise from the continuing tensions – between professional/managerial, professional/lay and local/central forms of power and control – which underpin the service. In particular, research indicates that many problems arise from the basic confusion about whether public involvement is driven by the operational need to enhance the quality of purchasing information or by a broader concern to improve the accountability of the organization (Cairncross and Ashburner 1992; Taylor and Lupton 1995). To develop a coherent strategy for public involvement, therefore, purchasers may need to replace the question of 'how to' with that of 'what for' – what is it that they want public involvement to achieve.

Fundamentally, such questions require purchasing agencies to identify the key principles and objectives underpinning their operation. For example, if purchasers are concerned about enhancing accountability, three central preconditions need to be met – ensuring the transparency of decision-making processes, demonstrating a preparedness to be held to account and indicating clearly where responsibility for decision making lies (see Chapter 3). These tenets of accountability relate to any public service, but its increased fragmentation and decentralization make them particularly difficult to operationalize within the NHS. The health service has always struggled with notions of accountability (Longley 1993; Klein 1995) and in particular with the tension between the central/local and managerial/professional lines of political accountability. The weakening of formal accountability at a local level, via the changes in the membership of health authority boards, the restricted role of the CHCs and local political representatives, has stimulated attempts to develop alternative methods of ensuring accountability. Although a substantial amount of *Local Voices* work has attempted to address these issues, it is clear that many health authorities continue to find this difficult and most general practitioners have yet to begin to address this agenda.

To determine the appropriate method to be used in public involvement, purchasers will need to develop a clear understanding of the broader policy or operational framework in which it takes place. Managing the interface between the public and purchasing successfully may involve the negotiation of national agendas – such as *Local Voices, Patient Partnership*, the *Accountability Framework* and *Delivering the Future* – as well as those deriving from the purchaser's local role as 'champion of the people'. It is likely to require the development of a multiplicity of approaches in order meet both purchaser and public expectations and to sustain activities within and between organizations. Figure 9.1 indicates the range of different approaches comprising the overall framework for public involvement. It also demonstrates the interplay between the consumerist/democratic and individualistic/collective approaches: the adoption of a community or collective approach may not automatically mean that such an approach is democratic in nature nor that mechanisms which involve the participation of individuals are necessarily consumerist in type. So, for example, while initiatives such as citizen juries may appear to involve a more collective approach, insofar as the views expressed are those of individuals and do not seek to be representative of the wider population, they are more appropriately viewed as consumerist in nature. Similarly, patient panels or participation groups draw on individual experience and involvement but, unlike citizen juries, have the potential to develop into more democratic forms of involvement. It is also clear that there are democratically-based activities, such as the act of voting in elections, which are centred on the role of individuals.

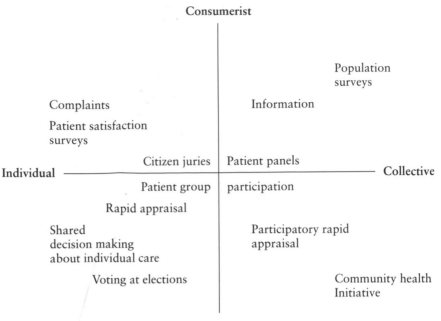

**Figure 9.1**  Frameworks for public involvement

Some approaches to public involvement incorporate a number of different dimensions of the wider framework. The structure and operation of the Community Health Councils, for example, may encompass a mixture of democratic and consumerist approaches to public involvement as well as the involvement of both individual patients and wider communities. To maximize the benefit of public involvement, the purchasing organization may need to combine a range of different methods and types of involvement, such that the limitations of each are mitigated by their combination with others – a 'methodological triangulation' approach to public involvement. Moreover, from a strategic standpoint, it may be necessary for the organization to approach public involvement as an ongoing and developmental process which moves through different stages or levels of involvement in a planned and coherent way, rather than the ad hoc 'pick-and-mix' approach developed by many purchasers over the 1990s (Lupton and Taylor 1995).

Over the past few years it is clear that the responsibility for public involvement has been shared between or has moved around, different locations within purchaser organizations, with public health, quality and communications departments taking some or all of the responsibility at various times (Taylor and Lupton 1995). With increasing pressures on management overheads and smaller purchasing agencies – especially at a primary care level – the development of specialist departments for public involvement may not be appropriate or possible. Purchasing organizations may thus need to examine new ways of managing public involvement activity. Before doing so, it may be important for them to consider one other important factor relating to the management of public involvement, that of its cost.

Rather surprising perhaps, there has been little interest in the literature on the relative costs of different methods of involvement or on the overall cost of this area of work to healthcare purchasers. Yet, to ensure the most effective use of resources, the costs of involvement will need to be set against the perceived benefits. Benefits, of course, can be measured in a number of ways depending whose perspective is taken – the public's or the healthcare purchaser's. The first major study to examine the costs of different approaches to public involvement was undertaken by Bowling *et al.* (1992) in the context of priority setting. They concluded that making contact with existing groups was the most cost-efficient way to gather consumer views when compared with other methods such as surveys or the use of more apparently sophisticated techniques. Although not cheap, this approach had the benefit of establishing two-way communication between the health authority and community groups. More recent work on citizens' juries has found them to be very expensive: on average around £12,000 each (Bower 1996). One of the pilot juries established by the King's Fund examined the problems of GP recruitment in 1996 at a cost over £20,000. Its conclusions were the same as those already reached by the health authority (Eltringham 1997). If confirmed more widely, this finding raises fundamental questions about the value for money of such exercises. It is interesting, moreover, to assess such costs against the overall spend by health purchasers on this area of activity. A study by Cooper *et al.* (1995) revealed that purchaser spending on community involvement ranged from £250 to £25,000 a year. Clearly, in this context, large-scale exercises will be prohibitive for most authorities, particularly the smaller primary care purchasers.

While the organizational and policy context of purchasing may be constantly changing, research indicates that there a number of basic management principles which will consistently need to be addressed by any purchasing agency (Taylor 1994; Taylor and Lupton 1995). Most importantly, it suggests that there should be a clear senior management responsibility for public involvement in order to ensure that it is taken forward strategically as well as at an operational/project level. Although many argue that it is necessary for everyone within the organization to own public involvement, it may nevertheless be essential that someone assumes overall responsibility. Wherever the organizational responsibility for public involvement ultimately lies it will be important to support staff through training, to commit adequate resources and to allow time for its development. Within the organization, there also need to be mechanisms for coordinating this activity which can relate to other approaches to public involvement, such as joint commissioning or joint work with providers. It may also be valuable to take a longer-term view of the goals of public involvement.

Centrally driven policy and guidance has tended to focus attention on short-term goals such as improved information-giving and a faster response to complaints. Better results, for both the public and purchasing organizations, may come from more sustained and developmental approaches to public involvement.

The purchasing organization should also create opportunities for its staff to meet the public in a range of settings and the systematic monitoring and regular review of public involvement initiatives will provide useful organizational learning. In particular, attention may need to be given to the different roles of public representatives/advocates/proxies and to identifying at what points in public involvement initiatives the different kinds of 'public' can be most helpful. As we have argued, it is essential that the organization itself is clear about its goals for public involvement and ensures that these are explicitly communicated. This will be of increasing importance in the hybrid provider–purchaser primary care organizations of the future. Not only is it important that organizations display transparency of purpose but they should also ensure that the results of public involvement initiatives are fed back to participants in ways that enable accountability for the decisions taken.

Finally, not least for reasons of cost, purchaser organizations may need to make more use of existing routes for public involvement. The benefits of tapping into the experience and advice of non-executive members and local and national voluntary sector agencies may be considerable. Workers in other statutory agencies may also have a wide experience and knowledge of public involvement which could be of value and prevent the reinvention or duplication of activities – a consideration of particular relevance for small primary care purchasers. It may be appropriate for purchasers to develop a specific responsibility for providing an independent and enduring infrastructure to support public and patient involvement. Research, particularly in relation to user involvement in community care, has demonstrated that good infrastructure arrangements are essential for promoting and supporting such involvement (DoH/KPMG 1992; McGrath and Grant 1992; Wistow 1992). Above all, purchasing organizations need to be clear about what they are doing and be realistic about what can be achieved through public involvement (Summers and McKeown 1996). In order to avoid dashed expectations, it is important to avoid setting too high a goal too quickly. Effective public involvement requires time to understand and negotiate different agendas, to undertake adequate planning, seek advice, develop adequate timescales and realistic expectations and to identify adequate resources.

## Future developments in the NHS

As we have argued, the central policy shift towards a primary care-led NHS raises important issues about the roles and functions of health authorities and primary care purchasers in relation to operational and strategic purchasing and to broader commissioning responsibilities. In the short term at least the continued development of hybrid purchaser–provider organizations will produce a multiplicity of organizational forms undertaking the purchasing of healthcare. Questions about where the organizational responsibility for public involvement will lie, and what priority it will have in respect to other pressures and priorities, will become central. As we have argued, the erosion of their direct purchasing role may shift health authorities more towards the role of 'market regulators', overseeing both purchasing and provider functions in a multilayered service. At the other end, there will be primary care-based organizations involved in purchasing healthcare services from themselves and other primary and secondary providers as well as undertaking more strategic purchasing functions.

It is possible that the further move towards locality based purchasing through collaborative arrangements in primary care – will counter the dominant individualism and provide a more population-focused approach to public involvement. This is not to devalue the importance of patient consultations as they can often be developed as effective methods of involvement (Hope 1996; Royal Pharmaceutical Society of Great Britain 1997) and may provide important purchasing information – a key point made by existing GP fundholders (Audit Commission 1996). However, as we have argued, purchasing agencies need to address wider community needs rather than simply respond to the individual needs revealed via patient consultations. To do so may require the development of alternative approaches to health needs assessment and additional, more collective, forms of public involvement.

The emphasis on localities has both political and organizational support. The locality can provide the point at which more strategic purchasing will occur and may also provide the optimum place for joint or alliance working – an important aspect of public involvement. The early experience of the Total Purchasing Projects (Total Purchasing National Evaluation Team 1997) suggests that general practice can and will develop liaison arrangements with other agencies such as social services and it is likely that voluntary and community groups will also find localities easier to work within given their development within the local government and joint planning framework of the 1970s and 1980s (see Chapter 5). The development of 'Health for All' initiatives, moreover, generated experience and understanding of local alliance working between local authorities and the NHS and the creation of Health Action Zones provides new opportunities for collaboration (DoH 1997b). Problems can occur, however, as a result of the lack of 'coterminosity', of different locality boundaries; this has been shown to affect detrimentally the processes of joint agency working (Exworthy and Peckham forthcoming). The existing development of primary care localities and multipractice purchasing arrangements, moreover, has paid little attention to the locality boundaries of other agencies or to the overlap between patient lists and local geographical boundaries.

The multilayered development of purchasing may also provide the answer to the central question about where the responsibility for public involvement will lie in the future. As we have argued, three distinct levels or types of purchasing emerged over the mid-1990s: individual practices or small primary care organizations at the first level; the larger primary care organizations or localities at the second level; and the health authorities at the third. The first two levels will in the future be integrated into the new Primary Care Groups. It may be appropriate for each of these different levels to develop a similarly distinctive responsibility for, and approach to, public involvement. Thus primary care purchasers would focus more on the individual aspects of involvement such as patient/health professional consultations, complaints and consumer feedback mechanisms and with some aspects of the broader public involvement agenda via work with other agencies, the public and existing voluntary and community sector organizations. The extent of public involvement will potentially increase as Primary Care Groups move from stage one (advisory role) to stage four (autonomous trust) (DoH 1997b). The health authorities would perform an overall strategic role by supporting infrastructures for public involvement, sharing expertise and experience across purchasing levels, ensuring that purchasers developed public involvement initiatives and supporting alliance or joint working between agencies. As confidence in their market management role grows, health authorities may engage in more comprehensive public involvement exercises on issues of importance across individual localities. Discharging this responsibility effectively, however, will require that health authorities engage with the broader roles and responsibilities of popular democratic as opposed to managerial accountability and begin to develop more participatory and collective mechanisms for involving the public more widely.

In many ways, therefore, the future of public involvement in healthcare purchasing stands at a crossroads. On the one hand, the strengthening of primary care purchasing makes the dominance of the consumerist approach, based on the individualistic (and unequal) relationship of doctor and patient, more likely, underpinned as it is by central government policy and directives. On the other, the decentralization of purchasing and the development by health authorities of a 'strategic regulator' role, possibly in conjunction with local authorities, may require the emergence of more democratic approaches to involving the public. Both these approaches are important in their different ways: the consumerist approach to ensure the responsiveness and operational accountability of particular services/agencies to individual consumers or service users; the democratic approach to provide for broader political accountability to the public as citizens, and members of wider communities. As we have argued above, moreover, particular activities deriving from either (or both) of the consumerist/democratic frameworks may be appropriate to the distinctive objectives of each of the different stages of Primary Care Group development and of the PCGs and the HA.

We have also indicated, however, that public involvement of whatever type costs time and resources to undertake effectively and increasingly may be seen as an optional extra on the part of purchasers struggling with other operational/policy objectives and in a context of restricted resources. It is necessary, therefore, to conclude this book by returning to the central question with which we started, and which has continued to trouble the NHS since its inception: the paradox of the public. Why should the public have a role in the provision of health or other public service and what is the appropriate nature of that role? The answer to this question is centrally related to wider questions about the nature and function of public sector services and, ultimately, to those concerning the kind of society in which we wish to live.

The involvement of the public in all areas of public services, but perhaps particularly in health, we have argued, is important for two central reasons. Firstly, because public services are more than the sum of personal choices made by self-interested individuals. Health is a public not a private good, in the sense that the health of the individual and the collectivity are intimately connected. Particularly in the context of scarce resources, the objectives and priorities surrounding access to healthcare have to be underpinned by common values and collective choices. To the extent that these are only inadequately represented by formal electoral processes, or by the fact of state funding, their achievement requires the active participation of the public in all its forms. Secondly, and relatedly, we argue that the act and process of public participation is important in itself. As Kawachi and Kennedy (1997) and others have argued, the physical health of a nation is closely related to the quality of its social capital. The participation of the public in the collective choices underpinning public services may provide a means of reinvigorating the common interests and ties of mutual dependence that are essential to countering the processes of social exclusion and fragmentation that increasingly characterize the societies in which we live. On the basis of such considerations, it becomes clear that the idea of public involvement cannot meaningfully be understood as a 'paradox' – 'a seemingly absurd or contradictory statement' – but rather the reverse: as we move towards the millenium, the active and informed participation of the public must be seen as the defining 'paradigm' for the future development of public sector services.

# Bibliography

Abelson, J., Lomas, J., Eyles, J. and Birch, S. (1995) 'Does the community want devolved authority? Results from deliberative polling in Ontario', *Canadian Medical Association Journal*, 153: 403–14.

ACHCEW (1986) *The Patient's Charter*. London: Association of Community Health Councils England and Wales.

Adonis, A. (1990) *Parliament Today*. Manchester: Manchester University Press.

Alford, R. (1975) *Health Care Politics*. Chicago: University of Chicago.

Allsop, J. (1995) *Health Policy in the NHS*. London: Longman.

Agass, M., Coulter, A., Mant, D. and Fuller, A. (1991) 'Patient participation in general practice: who participates?', *British Journal of General Practice*, 41, 198–201.

Appleby, J. (1994) 'The reformed National Health Service: a commentary', *Social Policy and Administration*, 28(4), 345–58.

Appleby, J., Robinson, R., Little, V. and Salter, J. (1990) 'The use of markets in the health service: The NHS reforms and managed competition', *Public Money and Management*, Winter, 27–33.

Appleby, J., Smith, P., Renade, W., Little, V. and Robinson, R. (1994) 'Monitoring managed competition', in R. Robinson and J. Le Grand (eds) *Evaluating the NHS Reforms*. London: Kings Fund Institute.

Arnstein, S. (1969) 'A ladder of citizen participation', *Journal of the American Institute of Planners*, 35(4), 216–224.

Ascher, K. (1987) *The Politics of Privatisation. Contracting out Public Services*. Basingstoke: Macmillan Education.

Ashton, J. and Seymour, H. (1988) *The New Public Health*. Milton Keynes: Open University Press.

Atkinson, R. (1996) 'Two modes of citizenship in contemporary British governance: consumerism and participation', paper presented at a seminar on *Good Governance*, Hong Kong, 18 April. City University, Division of Social Studies: Hong Kong.

Audit Commission (1993) *Protecting the Public Purse: Probity in the Public Sector: Combating Fraud and Corruption in Local Government*. London: HMSO.

Audit Commission (1996) *What the Doctor Ordered: A Study of GP Fundholders in England and Wales*. London: HMSO.

Bacon, R. and Eltis, W. (1976) *Britain's Economic Problem: Too Few Producers*. Basingstoke: Macmillan.

Bacharach, P. (1975) in J.R. Pennock and J.W. Chapman (eds) *Participation Politics*. New York: Leïber-Atherton.

Bailey, R. and Brake, M. (1975) *Radical Social Work*. London: Arnold.

Baldcock, J. and Ungerson, C. (1994) *Becoming Consumers of Community Care*. York: Joseph Rowntree Foundation.

Balogh, R. (1996) 'Exploring the role of localities in health commissioning: a review of the literature', *Social Policy & Administration*, 30(3), 99–113.

Barclay Committee (1982) *Social Workers: Their Roles and Tasks*. London: Bedford Square Press.

Barnard, S. (1995) *Whose Audit?: Consumer Involvement and Inter-agency Collaboration in Audit*. Social Services Research and Information Unit, Report no. 29. Portsmouth: SSRIU.

Barnes, M., Coumie, J. and Crichton, M. (1994) *User Panels – Representative Views from Frail Older People*. Scotland: Age Concern.

Barnes, M., Coumie, J. and Crichton, M. (1995) *Consumers, Citizens and Officials: New Relationships in Health and Social Care?* Leeds: Nuffield Institute for Health.

Barry, B. (1974) 'Exit, voice and loyalty', *British Journal of Political Science*, 4, 79–107.

Bartlett, W. and Harrison, S. (1993) 'Quasi-markets in the NHS', in J. Le Grand and W. Bartlett (eds) *Quasi-markets and Social Policy*. Basingstoke: Macmillan.

Barzelay, M. (1992) *Breaking Through Bureaucracy: A New Vision for Managing in Government*. Berkeley: University of California Press.

Bellamy, R. and Greenaway, J. (1995) 'The New Right conception of citizenship and The Citizen's Charter', *Government and Opposition*, 30, 469–91.

Bennington, J. (1978) *Local Government Becomes Big Business*. London: Community Development Project.

Beresford, P. and Croft, S. (1993) *Citizen Involvement: A Practical Guide for Change*. Basingstoke: Macmillan.

Berry, L. (1983) 'The rhetoric of consumerism and the exclusion of community', *Community Development Journal*, 23, 266–72.

Bevan, A. (1978) *In Place of Fear*. London: Quartet.

Beveridge Report (1942) *Interdepartmental Committee on Social Insurance and Allied Services*. Cmnd 6404. HMSO: London.

Beveridge, W. (1948) *Voluntary Action*. London: Allen and Unwin.

Boaden, N., Goldsmith, M., Hampton, W. and Stringer, P. (1982) *Public Participation in Local Services*. Harrow: Longman.

Bond, M. (1994) 'Getting the views of users and potential users', *Research, Policy and Planning*, 11(1/2) 24–31.

Booth, T.A. (ed.) (1979) *Planning for Welfare*. Oxford: Basil Blackwell and Martin Robertson.

Bosanquet, N. (1992) 'Interim report: the national health', in R. Jowell *et al.* (eds) *British Social Attitudes: The 9th Report*. London: Social and Community Planning Research.

Bower, H. (1996) 'Citizens have their say on health care', *British Medical Journal*, 313, 1164.

Bowling, A.S. (1994) *What People Say about Prioritizing Health Services*. London: King's Fund.

Bowling, A.S., Farquar, M., Fornby, J., McAllister, G., Kelly, R. and Shiner, M. (1992) *Local Voices in Purchasing Health Care. An Exploratory Exercise in Public Consultation on Priority Setting*. University of London: Needs Assessment Unit.

Bradshaw, J.S. (1972) 'A taxonomy of social need', in R. McLachlan (ed.) *Problems and Progress in Medical Care. Essays on Research Series*. London: Oxford University Press.

Brenton, M. (1985) *The Voluntary Sector in British Social Services*. London: Longman.

Brotchie, J. and Wann, M. (1993) *Training for Lay Participation in Health*. London: The Patients' Association.

Brown, I. (1994) 'Community and participation for general practice: perceptions of general practitioners and community nurses', *Social Science and Medicine*, 39(3), 335–43.

Burns, D., Hambeton, R. and Hoggett, P. (1993) *Politics of Decentralisation*. London: Macmillan.

Butler, J. (1992) *Patients, Policies and Politics. Before and After Working for Patients*. Buckingham: Open University Press.

Cabinet Office (1988) *Improving Management in Government: The Next Steps. A Report to the Prime Minister* (Ibbs Report). London: HMSO.

Cairncross, L. and Ashburner, L. (1992) 'Out of the bunker', *Health Service Journal*, 102(5293), 20–2.

Campbell, P. (1990) 'Mental health self-advocacy', in L. Winn (ed.) *Power to the People: The Key to Responsive Services in Health and Social Care*. London: Kings Fund.

Carers' Alliance (1989) *A Charter for Carers*. London: Carers' Alliance.

Carruthers, I., Fillingham, D., Ham, C.J. and James, J.H. (1995) *Purchasing in the NHS: The Story so Far*. Birmingham: Health Services Management Centre, University of Birmingham.

Cervie, B. and Cresswell, J. (1996) 'CHCs should work for HAs, consultants tell executive', *Health Service Journal*, 106(5330), 4.

Chandler, J. (1996) 'The United States of America', in A. Wall (ed.) *Health Systems in Liberal Democracies*. London: Routledge.

CAF (Charities Aid Foundation) (1992) *Charity Household Survey*. London: CAF.

Clarke, J. (1995) 'Public nightmares and communitarian dreams', in *Working Papers on Managerialism and Social Policy*. Milton Keynes: Open University.

Clarke, J. (1996) 'Capturing the customer: consumerism and social welfare', in *Working Papers on Managerialism and Social Policy*. Milton Keynes: Open University.

Clarke, M. and Stewart, J. (1986) *The Public Service Orientation: Issues and Dilemmas to be Faced*. Luton: Local Government Training Board.

Clarke, M. and Stewart, J. (1992) 'Empowerment: a theme for the 1990s', *Local Government Studies*, 18(2), 18–26.

Clode, D., Parker, C. and Etherington, S. (eds) (1987) *Towards the Sensitive Bureaucracy: Consumers, Welfare and the New Pluralism*. Aldershot: Gower.

Cooper, L., Cook, A., Davies, A. and Jackson, C. (1995) *Voices Off: Tackling the Democratic Deficit in Health*. London: Institute for Public Policy Research.

Cornwell, J. (1984) *Hard Earned Lives. Accounts of Health and Illness from* Γ *London.* London: Tavistock.

Coulter, A. (1995) 'Evaluating general practice fundholding in the United Kingdom', *European Journal of Public Health*, 5, 233–9.

Cox, D. (1991) 'Health service management – a sociological review: Griffiths and the non-negotiated order of the hospital', in J. Gabe, M. Calnan and M. Bury (eds) *The Sociology of the Health Service.* London: Routledge.

Cresswell, I. (1992) *Participatory Rapid Appraisal: An Investigation into Health and Social Needs of People Living in Danesmoor.* Chesterfield: North Derbyshire Health Authority.

Croft, S. and Beresford, P. (1989) 'User-involvement, citizenship and social policy', *Critical Social Policy*, 26, 5–18.

Crossman, R. (1976) 'The role of the volunteer in modern social service', in A. Halsey (ed.) *Tradition in Social Policy.* Oxford: Basil Blackwell.

Crouch, C. (1985) 'Exit and voice in the future of the welfare state', *Government and Opposition*, 20(3), 407–21.

Cutler, T. and Waine, B. (1994) *Managing the Welfare State.* Oxford: Berg.

Davis-Smith, J. (1992) 'What we know about volunteering. Information from the surveys', in R. Hedley and J. Davis-Smith (eds) *Volunteering and Society: Principles and Practice.* London: Bedford Square Press.

Day, P. and Klein, R. (1987) *Accountabilities: Five Public Services.* London: Tavistock.

Dearlove, J. (1973) *The Politics of Policy in Local Government.* Cambridge: Cambridge University Press.

Dennis, N. and Halsey, A.H. (1988) *English Ethical Socialism.* Oxford: Oxford University Press.

Department of the Environment (1991) Local Government Act 1988. Part I. Competition in the Provision of Local Authority Services. Circular 1/91. London: Department of the Environment.

Department of Health (1991) *The Patient's Charter.* London: HMSO.

Department of Health (1992a) *The Health of the Nation.* London: HMSO.

Department of Health (1992c–g) *Key Handbooks.* HMSO: London.

Department of Health (1995a) *The Health of the Nation: Tackling Variations in Health.* London: HMSO.

Department of Health (1995b) *Practical Guidance on Joint Commissioning for Project Leaders.* London: HMSO.

Department of Health (1995c) *The Second Patient's Charter.* London: HMSO.

Department of Health (1995d) *Acting on Complaints.* London: HMSO.

Department of Health (1996a) *Choice and Opportunity.* Cm 3390. London: HMSO.

Department of Health (1996b) *The National Health Service: A Service with Ambitions.* Cm 3425. London: HMSO.

Department of Health (1996c) *Primary Care: Delivering the Future.* Cm 3512. London: HMSO.

Department of Health/KPMG (1992) *Improving Independent Sector Involvement in Community Care Planning.* London: Department of Health/ KP Management Group.

Department of Health (1997a) *Developing Partnerships in Mental Health.* Green Paper. London: HMSO.

Department of Health (1997b) *The New NHS: Modern, Dependable.* Cm 3807. London: HMSO.

Department of Health (1998) *Our Healthier Nation.* London: HMSO.

Department of Health and Social Security (1968) *NHS: The Administrative Structure and the Medical and Related Services in England and Wales* [Green Paper]. London: HMSO.

Department of Health and Social Security (1969) *Report of the Committee of Enquiry into Allegations of Ill-treatment of Patients and other Irregularities at the Ely Hospital, Cardiff*. London: HMSO.

Department of Health and Social Security (1976) *The National Health Service Planning System*. London: HMSO.

Department of Health and Social Security (1979) *Royal Commission on the NHS*. Cmnd 7615 (Merrison Report). London: HMSO.

Department of Health and Social Security (1980) *Inequalities in Health* (Black Report) London: Department of Health and Social Security.

Department of Health and Social Security (1983) *NHS Management Enquiry* (Griffiths Report), DA (83) 38. London: HMSO.

Department of Health and Social Security (1987) *Promoting Better Health: The Government's Programme for Improving Primary Health Care*. Cm 248. London: HMSO.

Department of Health and Social Security and Welsh Office (1979) *Patients First: Consultative Document on the Structure and Management of the NHS in England and Wales*. Cm 555. London: HMSO.

Department of Health, Welsh Office, Scottish Home and Health Departments and Northern Ireland Office (1989a) *Working for Patients*. Cm 555. HMSO: London.

Department of Health, Welsh Office, Scottish Home and Health Departments and Northern Ireland Office (1989b) *Caring for People: Community Care in the Next Decade and Beyond*. Cm 849. HMSO: London.

Dixon, J. and Glennerster, H. (1995) 'What do we know about fundholding in general practice?', *British Medical Journal*, 311: 727–30.

Dixon, J. and Welch, H.G. (1991) 'Priority setting: lessons from Oregon'. *Lancet*, 337, 891–4.

Doern, G.B. (1993) 'The UK Citizen's Charter: origins and implementation in three agencies', *Policy and Politics*, 21(1), 17–29.

Doig, A. (1995) 'Mixed Signals? Public sector change and the proper conduct of public business', *Public Administration*, 73 (Summer), 191–212.

Doyal, L. and Gough, I. (1991) *A Theory of Human Need*. London: Macmillan.

du Gay, P. and Salaman, G. (1992) 'The cult(ure) of the customer', *Journal of Management Studies*, 29(5), 615–33.

Dun, R. (1989) *Pictures of Health*. London: West Lambeth HA.

Dun, R. (1991) 'Working with the voluntary sector', in A. McNaught (ed.) *Managing Community Health Services*. London: Chapman Hall.

Dunleavy, P. (1986) 'Explaining the privatisation boom: public choice versus radical approaches', *Public Administration*, 64, 13–34.

Dunleavy, P. (1991) *Democracy, Bureaucracy and Public Choice. Economic Explanations in Social Science*. London: Harvester Wheatsheaf.

Dunsire, A. (1990) 'The public–private debate: some UK evidence', *International Review of Administrative Sciences*, 56(1), 29–62.

Dynes, M. and Walker, D. (1995) *The New British State: The Government Machine in the 1990s*. London: Times Books.

Edwards, B. (1995) *The National Health Service: A Manager's Tale 1946–1994*. London: Nuffield Provincial Hospitals Trust.

Eltringham, D. (1997) Presentation on 'Citizen's juries' to Conference in Sheffield, 27 March.

Exworthy, M. and Peckham, S. (forthcoming) The contribution of coterminosity to joint purchasing in health and social care. *Health and Place*.

Fenwick, J. (1989) 'Consumerism and local government', *Local Government Policy Making*, 16(1), 45–52.

Finch, J. and Groves, D. (1983) *A Labour of Love: Women, Work and Caring*. London: Routledge and Kegan Paul.

Flynn, R., Grey, A. and Jenkins, W.I. (1990) 'Taking the next steps: the changing management of government', *Parliamentary Affairs*, 43(2), 159–78.

Flynn, R., Pickard, S. and Williams, G. (1995) 'Contracts and the quasi-market in community health services', *Journal of Social Policy*, 24(4), 529–50.

Flynn, R., Williams, G. and Pickard, S. (1996) *Markets and Networks: Contracting in Community Health Services*. Buckingham: Open University Press.

Foucault, M. (1977) *Discipline and Punish*. Harmondsworth: Penguin.

Friedman, M. and Friedman, R. (1980) *Free to Choose*. London: Warburg.

Friedman, M. and Friedman, R. (1985) *The Tyranny of the Status Quo* (revised edition). Harmondsworth: Penguin.

Friere, P. (1972) *The Pedagogy of the Oppressed*. Harmondsworth: Penguin.

Gann, R. and Buckland, S. (1996) *Disseminating Treatment Outcomes Information to Consumers*. London: King's Fund.

Ghazi, P. and Bevins, A. (1996) Now Only 'Yes Minister', *Observer*, 14 April.

Gilbert, N. and Gilbert, B. (1989) *The Enabling State*. New York: Oxford University Press.

Gillam, S.J. (1992) Assessing the health care needs of populations – the general practitioner's contribution. *British Journal of General Practice*, 42, 404–5.

Gladstone, F.L. (1979) *Voluntary Action in a Changing World*. London: Bedford Square Press.

Glennerster, H., Matsaganis, M., Owens, P. and Hancock, S. (1994) *Implementing GP Fundholding: Wild Card or Winning Hand?* Buckingham: Open University Press.

Goldsworthy, D. (1991) *Setting up Next Steps: A Short Account of the Origins, Launch and Implementation of the 'Next Steps Project' in the British Civil Service*. London: HMSO.

Gordon, P. and Hadley, J. (eds) (1996) *Extending Primary Care*. Oxford: Radcliffe Medical Press.

Grace, V.M. (1991) 'The marketing of empowerment and the construction of the health consumer: a critique of health promotion', *International Journal of Health Services*, 21(2), 329–43.

Gray, A. and Jenkins, B. (1993) 'Markets, managers and the public service: the changing of a culture', in P. Taylor-Gooby and R. Lawson (eds) *Markets and Managers*. Buckingham: Open University Press.

Gray, A., Jenkins, W., with Flyn, A. and Rutherford, B. (1991) 'The management of change in Whitehall: the experience of the FMI', *Public Administration*, 69(1), 41–59.

Green, D.G. (1987) *The New Right*. Brighton: Wheatsheaf.

Green, D.G. (1990) *The NHS Reforms: Whatever Happened to Consumer Choice?* London: Institute of Economic Affairs.

Griffiths, R. (1988) *Community Care: Agenda for Action*. London: HMSO.

Guillebaud (1956) *Report of the Committee of Enquiry into the Cost of the NHS*. Cmnd 9663. London: HMSO.

Gyford, J. (1991) *Citizens, Consumers and Councils*. London: Macmillan.

Hadley, R. and Hatch, S. (1981) *Social Welfare and the Failure of the State*. London: George Allen and Unwin.

Hallett, C. (1987) *Critical Issues in Participation*. Newcastle: Association of Community Workers.

Ham, C. and Spurgeon, P. (1992) *Effective Purchasing*. Birmingham: Health Services Management Centre.

Ham, C. (1994) 'Think globally, act locally', *Health Service Journal*, 104(5385), 27–8.

Ham, C. (1996) 'Population centred and patient focused purchasing – the UK experience', *Millbank Quarterly*, 74(2), 191–7.

Hambleton, R. (1988) 'Consumerism, decentralisation and local democracy', *Public Administration*, 66 (Summer), 125–47.

Hamilton-Gurney, B. (1995) *Public Participation in Health Care*. Health Services Research Group. Cambridge: University of Cambridge.

Harden, I. (1992) *The Contracting State*. Buckingham: Open University Press.

Harris, A. (1996) *Needs Assessment in General Practice*. London: Churchill Livingstone.

Harris, A. (ed.) (1997) *Needs to Know: A Guide to Needs Assessment for Primary Care*. London: Churchill Livingstone.

Harrison, S., Hunter, D.J. and Pollitt, C.J. (1990) *The Dynamics of British Health Policy*. London: Unwin Hyman.

Harrison, S. and Pollitt, C. (1994) *Controlling Health Professionals*. Buckingham: Open University Press.

Harrison, S. (1997) 'Central government should have a greater role in rationing decisions: the case against', *British Medical Journal*, 314, 970–3.

Hastings, A. and Rashid, A. (1993) General practice in deprived areas: problems and solutions. *British Journal of General Practice*, 43, 47–51.

Hatch, S. (ed.) (1983) *Volunteers: Patterns, Meanings and Motives*. Berkhamsted: The Volunteer Centre.

Hayek, F.A. (1960) *The Constitution of Liberty*. London: RKP.

Hayek, F.A. (1984) *Unemployment and the Unions*. Hobart Paper no. 87. London: IEA.

Health Service Journal (1994) 'Private sector has boomed', *Health Service Journal*, 104, 3.

Heritage, Z. (1994) *Community Participation in Primary Care*. London: Royal College of General Practitioners.

Hirschman, A.O. (1970) *Exit, Voice and Loyalty: Responses to Decline in Firms, Organisations and States*. Cambridge, Mass.: Harvard University Press.

Hogg, C. (1995) *Beyond The Patient's Charter*. London: Health Rights.

Hoggett, P. (1992) *The Politics of Empowerment. The Decentralisation Bulletin*, no. 1. Bristol: University of Bristol, School of Advanced Urban Studies.

Honigsbaum, F. (1989) *Health, Happiness and Security: The Creation of the National Health Service*. London: Routledge.

Honigsbaum, F., Richards, J. and Lockett, T. (1995) *Priority Setting in Action: Purchasing Dilemmas*. Oxford: Radcliffe Medical Press.

Hood, C. (1991) 'A public management for all seasons?', *Public Administration*, 69 (Spring), 3–19.

Hood, C. (1991) 'Stabilisation and cutbacks: a catastrophe for government growth theory?', *Journal of Theoretical Politics*, 3(1), 37–63.

Hood, C. (1995) 'Contemporary public management: a new global paradigm?', *Public Policy and Administration*, 10(2), 104–7.

Hope, T. (1996) *Evidence-Based Patient Choice*. London: King's Fund.

House of Commons Committee of Public Accounts (1987) *Thirteenth Report: The Financial Management Initiative*. London: HMSO.

Hudson, B. (1992) 'Quasi-markets in health and social care in Britain: can the public sector respond?', *Policy and Politics*, 20(2), 131–42.

Hudson, B. (1997) 'Waiting in the wings', *Health Service Journal*, 107(5545), 34–5.

Hunt, G. (1990) ''Patient Choice' and the National Health Service Review', *Journal of Social Welfare Law*, 4, 245–55.

Hunter, D. and Harrison, S. (1993) *Effective Purchasing for Health Care: Proposals for the First Five Years*. Leeds: Nuffield Institute.

Hutton, W. (1996) 'Raising the stakes', *The Guardian*, 17 January, 3–4.

Ignatieff, M. (1989) 'Citizenship and moral narcissism', *Political Quarterly*, 60, 63–74.

Jobling, R. (1990) 'Reins tighten up for future CHCs', *Health Service Journal*, 100(5198), 278.

Johnson, N. (1989) 'The privatisation of welfare', *Social Policy and Administration*, 23(1), 17–32.

Johnson, N. (ed.) (1995) *Private Markets in Health and Welfare. An International Perspective*. Oxford: Berg.

Johnson, T.J. (1972) *Professions and Power*. Basingstoke: Macmillan.

Jones, J. and MacDonald, J. (1993) 'Editorial: who controls health care?', *Community Development Journal*, 28(3), 199–205.

Kawachi, I. and Kennedy, B.P. (1997) 'Health and social cohesion: why care about income inequality?', *British Medical Journal*, 314, 1037–40.

Kendall, I. and Moon, G. (1994) Health policy and the Conservatives, in S. Savage, R. Atkinson and L. Robins (eds) *Public Policy in Britain*. Basingstoke: Macmillan.

Kenner, C. (1986) *Whose Health is it Anyway?* London: Bedford Square Press.

Kenner, C. (1986) *Whose Needs Count? Community Action For Health*. London: Bedford Square Press.

Kettlewell, H. (1988) 'Consulting women in the community about local government services'. *Critical Social Policy*, 21 (Spring), 55–67.

Klein, R. (1971) 'Accountability in the health service', *Political Quarterly*, (42), 363–75.

Klein, R. (1980) 'Models of man and models of policy: reflections on "Exit, Voice and Loyalty" ten years later', *Health and Society*, 58(3), 416–29.

Klein, R. (1983) 'The private government of public health', in R. Maxwell and V. Morrison, *Working with People*. London: King Edward's Hospital Fund for London.

Klein, R. (1984) 'The politics of participation', in R. Maxwell and N. Weaver (eds) *Public Participation in Health*. London: King Edward's Hospital Fund for London.

Klein, R. (1989) *The Politics of the National Health Service*, 2nd edn. London: Longman.

Klein, R. (1990a) 'New lamps for old', *Health Service Journal*, 100(5211), 1110–11.

Klein, R. (1990b) 'Looking after consumers in the new NHS', *British Medical Journal*, 300, 1351–2.

Klein, R. (1991) 'On the Oregon trail: rationing health care', *British Medical Journal*, 302, 1–2.

Klein, R. (1995) *The New Politics of the National Health Service.* Hounslow: Longman.

Klein, R., Day, P. and Redmayne, S. (1996) *Managing Scarcity: Priority Setting and Rationing in the NHS,* Buckingham: Open University Press.

Klein, R. and Lewis, J. (1976) *The Politics of Consumer Representation. A Study of Community Health Councils.* London: Centre for Studies in Social Policy.

King's Fund Centre (1993) *Implementing Community Care: Consumer Participation in Community Care; Action for Managers.* London: NHS Training Directorate.

Laffin, M. (1986) *Professionalism and Policy: The Role of the Professions in the Central–Local Government Relationship.* Aldershot: Gower.

Leat, D. (1977) *Towards a Definition of Volunteering.* Berkhamsted: The Volunteer Centre.

Leathard, A. (1990) *Health Care Provision. Past, Present and Future.* London: Chapman and Hall.

Leonard, P. and Corrigan, P. (1978) *Social Work Practice Under Capitalism.* London: Macmillan.

Lewis, N. and Longley, D. (1992) 'Accountability in education, social services and health', paper to the European Policy Forum, *Accountability to the Public.* London: European Policy Forum.

Le Grand, J. and Bartlett, W. (eds) (1993) *Quasi-Markets and Social Policy.* Basingstoke: Macmillan.

Lindow, V. (1991) 'Experts, lies and stereotypes', *Health Service Journal,* 101, 18–19.

Lindow, V. (1993) *User Participation in Community Care.* London: Department of Health, Community Care Support Force.

Locke, J. (1947) 'An essay concerning the true, original extent and end of civil government', in E. Barker (ed.) *Social Contract.* Oxford: Oxford University Press.

Longley, D. (1993) *Public Law and Health Service Accountability.* Buckingham: Open University Press.

Lukes, S. (1974) *Power: A Radical View.* Basingstoke: Macmillan.

Lupton, C. and Hall, B. (1993) 'Beyond the rhetoric: from policy to practice in user-involvement', *Research, Policy and Planning,* 10(2), 6–11.

Lupton, C. and Raison, B. (1993) *User involvement: the view from service users.* SSRIU Occasional Paper no. 22. Portsmouth: Social Services Research and Information Unit, University of Portsmouth.

Lupton, C., Buckland, S. and Moon, G. (1995) 'Consumer involvement in health care purchasing: the role and influence of the community health councils', *Health and Social Care in the Community,* 3(4), 215–26.

Lupton, C. and Taylor, P. (1995) 'Coming in from the cold? Building public involvement into purchasing', *Health Service Journal,* 105(5444), 22–4.

Lupton, C. and Taylor, P. (1997) *Public Involvement in Healthcare Purchasing: Phase 2.* SSRIU Occasional Paper No 44. Portsmouth: Social Services Research and Information Unit, University of Portsmouth.

MacDonald, J. (1993) *Primary Health Care.* London: Earthscan Publications.

McGrath, M. (1989) 'Consumer participation in service planning – the AWS experience', *Journal of Social Policy,* 18(1), 67–89.

McGrath, M. and Grant, G. (1992) 'Supporting "needs-led" services: implications for planning and management systems (a case study in mental handicap services)', *Journal of Social Policy,* 21(1), 71–98.

McIvor, S. (1991) *Obtaining Views of Users of the Health Services.* London: King's Fund.

McVicar, M. and Robins, L. (1994) 'Education policy: market forces or market failure?', in S. Savage, A. Atkinson and L. Robins (eds) *Public Policy in Britain*. Basingstoke: Macmillan.

Marr, A. (1995) *Ruling Britannia*. London: Penguin.

Marsh, D. (1991) 'Privatisation under Mrs Thatcher: a review of the literature', *Public Administration*, 69 (Winter), 459–80.

Marshall, T.H. (1950) *Citizenship and Social Class and Other Essays*. Cambridge: Cambridge University Press.

Marshall, T.H. (1965) *Social Policy in the Twentieth Century*. London: Hutchinson University Library.

Massey, A. (1993) *Managing the Public Sector. A Comparative Analysis of the United Kingdom and the United States*. Aldershot: Edward Elgar.

Massey, A. (1995a) 'Civil service reform and accountability', *Public Policy and Administration*, 10(1), 16–33.

Massey, A. (1995b) 'Ministers, the agency model, and policy ownership', *Public Policy and Administration*, 10(2), 71–87.

Maxwell, R. and Morrison, V. (eds) (1983) *Working with People*. London: King Edward's Hospital Fund for London.

Maxwell, R. and Weaver, N. (eds) (1984) *Public Participation in Health*. London: King Edward's Hospital Fund for London.

Meade, K. and Carter, T. (1990) 'Empowering older users: some starting points', in L. Winn (ed.) *Power to the People*. London: King's Fund.

Mechanic, D. (1972) *Public Expectations and Health Care*. New York: John Wiley.

*MedEconomics* (1997) Special report on Labour Party proposals. *MedEconomics*, 18(1), 31–47.

Meleis, A.I. (1992) 'Community participation and involvement: theoretical and empirical issues', *Health Services Management Research*, 5(1), 5–16.

Mill, J.S. (1962) *Representative Government*. London: Dent, Everyman's Library.

Millar, B. (1996) 'On goes the muzzle', *Health Service Journal*, 106(5331), 11.

Ministry of Health (1944) *A National Health Service*. Cmnd 6502. London: HMSO.

Mishra, R. (1984) *The Welfare State in Crisis: Social Thought and Social Change*. Hemel Hempstead: Harvester Wheatsheaf.

Mohan, J. and Woods, K. (1985) 'Restructuring health care: the social geography of public and private health care under the British Conservative government', *International Journal of Health Services*, 15(2), 197–215.

Montgomery, J. (1992) Rights to health and health care, in A. Coote (ed.) *The Welfare of Citizens: Developing New Social Rights*. London: Institute of Public Policy Research.

Moon, G. and Lupton, C. (1995) 'Within acceptable limits: health care provider perspectives on community health councils in the reformed NHS', *Policy and Politics*, 23(4), 335–46.

Moore, J. (1987) *The Welfare State: The Way Ahead*. London: Conservative Political Centre.

Morcroft, I. (1989) *Collaboration in Planning and Working: The Voluntary Sector, Local Authorities and Health Authorities*. ARVAC (Association of Researchers in Voluntary Action and Community Involvement) Occasional Paper no. 10. London: London School of Economics.

Morris, J. and Lindow, V. (1993) *User Participation in Community Care Services*. London: DoH/Community Care Support Force.

Mullen, P. (1990) 'Which internal market? The NHS White Paper and internal markets', *Financial Accountability and Management*, 6, 33–50.

Murray, S.A., Tapson, J., Turnbull, L., McCallum, J. and Little, A. (1994) 'Listening to local voices: adapting rapid appraisal to assess health and social needs in general practice', *British Medical Journal*, 308, 698–700.

Murray, S. (ed.) (1996) *Needs Assessment in General Practice*. London: Royal College of General Practitioners.

NAHAT (1993) *Listening to Local Voices*, Research Paper no. 9. Birmingham: National Association of Health Authorities and Trusts.

Nairne, P. (1984) 'Parliamentary control and accountability', in R. Maxwell and N. Weaver (eds) *Public Participation in Health*. London: King Edward's Hospital Fund for London.

National Audit Office (1989) *Department of Employment: Provision of Training Through Managing Agents*, 569. London: HMSO.

NAWCH (1984) *The Charter for Children in Hospital*. London: National Association for the Welfare of Children in Hospital.

NCVO (1981) *Working Together: Partnerships in Local Social Services*. National Council for Voluntary Organisations. London: Bedford Square Press.

Neave, H. (1994) Community Assessment in General Practice. MSc Dissertation. University of Bristol.

NHSE (1994) *Developing NHS Purchasing: Toward a Primary Care Led NHS*. London: NHS Executive.

NHSE (1995a) *Accountability Framework for GP Fundholders*. London: NHS Executive.

NHSE (1995b) *Planning Guidelines*. London: NHS Executive.

NHSE (1996a) *Patient Partnership*. London: NHS Executive.

NHSE (1996b) *Promoting Clinical Effectiveness*. Leeds: NHS Executive.

NHSE (1996c) *Primary Care: The Future*. London: NHS Executive.

NHSE (1997a) *EL(97)33*. London: HMSO.

NHSE (1997b) *EL(97)37*. London: HMSO.

NHSE (1997c) *Priorities and Planning Guidance for the NHS: 1997/98*. Leeds: NHS Executive.

NHSME (1990) *Briefing Pack for NHS Managers*. London. NHS Management Executive.

NHSME (1992) *Local Voices. The Views of Local People in Purchasing for Health*. London: NHS Management Executive.

NHSME (1993) *Purchasing for Health: A Framework for Action*. Leeds: NHS Management Executive.

NHSME (1994) *Private Enterprise Governance in the NHS. Report of the Corporate Governance Task Force*. Leeds: NHS Management Executive.

Niskanen, W.A. (1971) *Bureaucracy and Representative Government*. New York: Aldine Atherton.

North, N. (1995) 'Alford revisited: the professional monopolisers, corporate rationalisers, community and markets', *Policy and Politics*, 23(2), 115–25.

Office of Public Management (1992) *The Climbing Frame*. London: HMSO.

Office of Public Census and Surveys (1987) *General Household Survey*. London: OPCS.

Oliver, M. (1990) *The Politics of Disablement*. London: Macmillan.

Ottewill, R. and Wall, A. (1990) *The Growth and Development of the Community Health Services*. Newcastle: Business Education Publishers.

Øvretveit, J. (1995) *Purchasing for Health*. Buckingham: Open University Press.
Owen, D. (1965) *English Philanthropy 1660–1960*. New York: Harvard University Press.
PAC (1993–4) *26th Report. Committee of Public Accounts*. HC295. London: HMSO.
Packwood, T., Buxton, M. and Keen, J. (1990) 'Resource management in the National Health Service: a first case history', *Policy and Politics*, 18(4), 245–65.
Papadakis, E. and Taylor-Gooby, P. (1987) 'Consumer attitudes and participation in state welfare', *Political Studies*, 35, 467–81.
Peckham, S. (1994) 'Local voices in primary care', *Critical Public Health*, 5(2), 36–40.
Peckham, S., MacDonald, J. and Taylor, P. (1996) *Towards a Public Health Model of Primary Care*. Birmingham: Public Health Alliance.
Percy-Smith, J. (ed.) (1996) *Needs Assessment in Public Policy*. Buckingham: Open University Press.
Petersen, A. (1996) 'The healthy city: expertise and the regulation of space', *Health and Place*, 2(3), 157–65.
Piette, D. (1990) Community participation in formal decision-making mechanisms. *Health Promotion International*, 187–197.
Pirie, M. (1985) *Privatisation*. London: Adam Smith Institute.
Pirie, M. (1991) *The Citizen's Charter*. London: Adam Smith Institute.
Plant, R. (1988) 'Citizenship, rights and socialism', *Fabian Tract*, 531, 1–20.
Plant, R. (1992) 'Citizenship, rights and welfare', in A. Coote (ed.) *The Welfare of Citizens. Developing New Social Rights*. London: Rivers Oram.
Plowden Report (1969) *Children and their Primary Schools*. London: Central Advisory Council for Education, HMSO.
Plummer, J. (1994) *The Governance Gap – Quangos and Accountability*. York: Joseph Rowntree Foundation.
Pollitt, C. (1988a) 'Editorial: consumerism and beyond', *Public Administration*, 66(2), 121–4.
Pollitt, C. (1988b) 'Bringing consumers into performance measurement: concepts, consequences and constraints', *Policy and Politics*, 16(2), 77–87.
Pollitt, C. (1990) *Managerialism and the Public Services: The Anglo-American Experience*. Oxford: Basil Blackwell.
Pollitt, C. (1994) ' "The Citizen's Charter": a preliminary analysis', *Public Money and Management*. April/June, 9–14.
Pollitt, C., Harrison, S., Hunter, D.J. and Murdock, J.G. (1991) 'General management in the NHS: the initial impact 1983–88', *Public Administration*, 69 (Spring), 61–83.
Potter, J. (1988) 'Consumerism and the public sector: how well does the coat fit?', *Public Administration*, 66 (Summer), 149–64.
Powell, M. (1996) 'Granny's footsteps, fractures and the principles of the NHS', *Critical Social Policy*, 47(16), 27–44.
Prime Minister's Office (1991) *Citizen's Charter: Raising the Standard*. Cm 1599. London: HMSO.
Pritchard, P. (1994) 'Community involvement in a changing world', in Z. Heritage (ed.) *Community Participation in Primary Care*. London: Royal College of General Practitioners.
Prowle, M. (1992) *Purchasing in the NHS: A Managerial Perspective*. Bristol: School of Advanced Urban Studies Publications, University of Bristol.
Public Health Alliance (1991) *Community Development and Health*. Birmingham: Public Health Alliance.

Ranade, W. (1995) 'The theory and practice of managed competition in the National Health Service', *Public Administration*, 73 (Summer), 241–62.

Ranson, S. and Stewart, J. (1989) 'Citizenship and government: the challenge for management in the public domain', *Political Studies*, 37, 5–24.

Ranson, S. and Stewart, J. (1994) *Management for the Public Domain: Enabling the Learning Society*. Basingstoke: Macmillan.

Rao, N. (1991) *From Providing to Enabling. Local Authorities and Community Care Planning*. York: Joseph Rowntree Foundation.

Rayner, G. (1986) 'Health care as a business?: the emergence of a commercial hospital sector in Britain', *Policy and Politics*, 14(4), 439–59.

Redcliffe-Maud Report (1969) *Royal Commission on Local Government in England*. Cmnd 4040. London: HMSO.

Redmayne, S. (1992) 'Skin deep', *Health Service Journal*, 102(5325), 28–9.

Redmayne, S. (1995) *Reshaping the NHS: Strategies, Priorities and Resource Allocation*. Research Paper no. 16. Birmingham: National Association of Health Authorities and Trusts.

Redmayne, S. (1996) *Small Steps, Big Goals*. Birmingham: National Association of Health Authorities and Trusts.

Redmayne, S., Klein, R. and Day, P. (1993) *Sharing out Resources: Purchasing and Priority Setting in the NHS*. Birmingham: National Association of Health Authorities and Trusts.

Rees, A.M. (1990) *Selecting Health Authority Members: Lessons from the Wessex Experience*. Southampton: Institute for Health Policy Studies, University of Southampton.

Rhodes, R.A.W. (1987) 'Developing public service orientation or "Let's add a soupçon of political theory"', *Local Government Studies*, May/June, 63–73.

Richardson, A. (1983) *Participation*. London: Routledge and Kegan Paul.

Richardson, A., Charnay, M., Hammer-Lloyd, S. (1992) 'Public opinion and purchasing', *British Medical Journal*, 304, 690–2.

Robb, B. (1967) *Sans Everything*. London: Nelson.

Robinson, R. and Le Grand, J. (1994) *Evaluating the NHS Reforms*. London: King's Fund.

Robinson, R. and Le Grand, J. (1995) 'Contracting and the purchaser–provider split', in R. Saltman and C. van Otter (eds) *Implementing Planned Markets in Health Care*. Buckingham: Open University Press.

Roche, M. (1987) 'Citizenship, social theory, and social change', *Theory and Society*, 16, 363–99.

Rosenthal, M.M. (1983) Neighbourhood health projects – some new approaches to health and community work in parts of the UK. *Community Development Journal*, 18(2), 120–31.

Rosenthal, M.M. (1995) *The Incompetent Doctor*. Buckingham: Open University Press.

Royal Commission (1979) *Royal Commission on the National Health Service Report*. Cmnd 7615. London: HMSO.

RPSGB (1997) *From Competition to Concordance: Achieving Shared Goals in Medicine Taking*. London: Royal Pharmaceutical Society of Great Britain.

Rutt, H. (1992a) *Rapid Appraisal*. St Albans: North West Hertfordshire Community Health Council.

Rutt, H. (1992b) *Maldon Rapid Appraisal*. St Albans: North West Hertfordshire Community Health Council.

Salisbury, C.J. (1989) 'How do people choose their doctor?', *British Medical Journal*, 299, 608–10.

Salter, B. (1995) 'The private sector and the NHS: redefining the welfare state', *Policy and Politics*, 23(1), 17–30.

Saltman, R. and von Otter, C. (eds) (1995) *Implementing Planned Markets in Health Care*. Buckingham: Open University Press.

Sang, B. (1984) 'Citizen advocacy in the United Kingdom – a first attempt', in B. Sang and J. O'Brien, *Advocacy: the UK and American Experiences*. King's Fund Project Paper no. 51. London: King Edward's Hospital Fund for London.

Scott-Samuel, A. (1989) 'The new public health? Speke neighbourhood health group', in D. Seedhouse and A. Cribb (eds) *Changing Ideas in Healthcare*. London: John Wiley and Sons.

Secretaries of State for Health, Wales, Northern Ireland and Scotland (1989) *Caring for People: Community Care in the Next Decade and Beyond*. Cm 8849. London: HMSO.

Seebohm Report (1968) *Report of the Committee on Local Authority and Allied Personal Social Services*. Cmnd 3703 London: HMSO.

Seldon, A. (1968) *After the NHS?*. Occasional Paper 21. London: Institute for Educational Analysis.

Seligman, M.E.P. (1972) 'Learned helplessness', *Annual Review of Medicine*, 23, 407–12.

Servian, R. (1996) Perceptions of Power. Master's Thesis. Bristol: University of Bristol.

Shackley, P. and Ryan, M. (1994) 'What is the role of the consumer in health care?', *Journal of Social Policy*, 23(4), 517–41.

SHIP (1992) *Charter for People in Pain*. London: Self Help in Pain.

Skeffington Report (1969) *People and Planning*. London: HMSO.

Skelcher, C. (1993) 'Involvement and empowerment in local public services', *Public Money and Management*, 13(3), 13–20.

Smith, C. (1996) in D. Brindle (ed.) 'Cradle to grave contract rewritten', *Guardian*, 8 May, 4.

Smith, R., Butler, F. and Powell, M. (1996) *Total Purchasing: a Model for Locality Commissioning*. Oxford: Radcliffe Medical Press.

Smithies, J. (1992) 'The public as partners: a tool box for involving people in commissioning health care'. Paper presented at the East Anglian RHA Health Gain Conference, Cambridge, East Anglian RHA, October.

Sockett, H.T. (ed.) (1980) *Accountability in the English School System*. London: Hodder and Stoughton.

Squires, J. (1994) *The Cracked Mirror: The Future for Representation*. London: Demos.

Stacey, M. (1976) 'The health service consumer: a sociological misconception', in M. Stacey (ed.) *Sociology of the NHS*. Sociological Review Monograph no. 22. Keele: University of Keele.

Stevens, A. and Gabbay, J. (1991) 'Needs assessment, needs assessment . . .', *Health Trends*, 23, 20–3.

Stewart, J.D. (1992) 'The rebuilding of public accountability', paper to the European Policy Forum, *Accountability to the Public*. London: European Policy Forum.

Stewart, J. and Clarke, M. (1987) 'The public service orientation: issues and dilemmas', *Public Administration*, 65(2), 161–77.

Stewart, J. and Walsh, K. (1992) 'Change in the management of public services', *Public Administration*, 70 (Winter), 499–518.

Stewart, J., Kendall, E. and Coote, A. (1995) *Citizen Juries*. London: Institute for Public Policy Research.

Stewart, J., Lewis, N. and Longley, D. (1992) European Policy Forum Paper. *Accountability to the Public*. London: European Policy Forum.

Stewart-Brown, S., Gillan, S. and Jewell, T. (1996) 'The Problems of Fundholding', *British Medical Journal*, 312, 1311–12.

Stoker, G. (1988) *The Politics of Local Government*. Basingstoke: Macmillan.

Strong, P. and Robinson, J. (1990) *The NHS Under New Management*. Milton Keynes: Open University Press.

Summers, A. and McKeown, K. (1996) 'Local voices: evolving a realistic strategy on public consultation', *Public Health*, 110, 145–50.

Sykes, W., Collins, M., Hunter, D., Popay, J. and Williams, G. (1992) *Listening to Local Voices: A Guide to Research Methods*. Leeds: Nuffield Institute for Health Service Studies.

Taylor, M., Hayes, L., Lart, R. and Mears, R. (1990) *User Empowerment in Community Care: Unravelling the Issues*. Bristol: School of Advanced Urban Society, University of Bristol and Joseph Rowntree Foundation.

Taylor, P. (1993) *What's in a Word? Consumer Involvement Project*. Swindon: Wiltshire Health Authority.

Taylor, P. (1995) *Public/Consumer Involvement: Developing a Strategy. Consumer Involvement Project*. Swindon: Wiltshire Health Authority.

Taylor, P. and Lupton, C. (1995) *Consumer Involvement in Health Care Commissioning*. Report no 30. Portsmouth: Social Services Research and Information Unit, University of Portsmouth.

Taylor, P. and Martin, T. (eds) (1995) *Consumer and Public Involvement: Directory of Reports and Resources Available in the South and West Region*. Portsmouth: South & West Regional Development Agenda, Social Services Research and Information Unit, University of Portsmouth.

Taylor-Gooby, P. (1991) 'Attachment to the welfare state', in R. Jowell, L. Brook and B. Taylor (eds) *British Social Attitudes: The Eighth Report*. Aldershot: Gower.

Thomas, D. (1978) 'Learning and change in community groups', *Group work: Learning and Practice*. NISW Paper no. 33. London: National Institute for Social Work.

Thunhurst, C. (1991) 'Information and Public Health', in P. Draper (ed.) *Health Through Public Policy*. London: Merlin Press.

Total Purchasing National Evaluation Team (1997) *Total Purchasing: A Profile of National Pilot Projects*. London: King's Fund.

Towell, D. (1988) *An Ordinary Life in Practice*. London: King Edward's Hospital Fund for London.

Towell, D. and Beardshaw, V. (1991) *Enabling Community Integration*. London. King's Fund.

Townsend, P. (1990) 'Individual or social responsibility for premature death. The current controversies in the British debate about health', *International Journal of Health Services*, 20(3), 373–92.

Townsend, P., Phillimore, D. and Beattie, A. (1987) *Health and Deprivation: Inequality and the North*. London: Croom Helm.

Ungerson, C. (1985) *Women and Social Policy*. London: Macmillan.

User Centred Services Group (1993) *Building Bridges Between People who Use and People who Provide Services*. London: National Institute of Social Work.

Vickridge, R. (1995) 'NHS reform and community care – means-tested health care masquerading as consumer choice?', *Critical Social Policy*, 15(1), 76–80.

Wall, A. (1995) 'Nightmare', *Health Service Journal*, 105(5481), 24–6.

Wall, A. (ed.) (1996) *Health Systems in Liberal Democracies*. London: Routledge.

Walsh, K. (1991) 'Citizens and consumers: marketing and public sector management', *Public Money and Management*, Summer, 9–16.

Walsh, K. (1995) *Public Services and Market Mechanisms: Competition, Contracting and the New Public Management*. Basingstoke: Macmillan Press.

Webb, A. and Wistow, G. (1986) *Planning, Need and Scarcity: Essays on the Personal Social Services*. London: Allen and Unwin.

Wessex Purchaser Development Programme (1993a) *The Climbing Frame: Steps Towards Effective Consumer and Public Involvement in Health Commissioning*. London: Office of Public Management.

Wessex Purchaser Development Programme (1993b) *Consumer and Public Involvement in Health Commissioning: Learning from the Experience in Bournemouth and Portsmouth*. London: Office of Public Management.

Whitehead, M. (1994) 'Is it fair? Evaluating the early Implications of the NHS reforms', in R. Robinson and J. Le Grand, *Evaluating the NHS Reforms*. London: Kings Fund.

Whittaker, A. (ed.) (1989) *Supporting Self Advocacy*. London: King's Fund.

Wilkinson, R. (1997) 'Health Inequalities: relative or absolute material standards?', *British Medical Journal*, 314, 591–5.

Williamson, C. (1992) *Whose Standards?: Consumer and Professional Standards in Health Care*. Buckingham: Open University Press.

Wilson, G. (1993) 'Users and providers: different perspectives on community care services', *Journal of Social Policy*, 22(4), 508–25.

Williams, S. (1996) *Fundholding 1996*. Beckenham: Publishing Initiatives Books.

Wiltshire Development Forum (1992) *Code of Good Practice on Consultation*. Devizes: Wiltshire Development Forum.

Winn, L. (1990) *Power to the People – The Key to Responsive Services in Health and Social Care*. London: King's Fund.

Winkler, F. (1987) 'Consumerism in health care: beyond the supermarket model', *Policy and Politics*, 15(1), 1–8.

Wistow, G. (1990) *Community Care Planning: A Review of Past Experiences and Future Imperatives*. London: Department of Health.

Wistow, G. (1992) 'Working together in a new policy concept', *Health Services Management*, 88(2), 25–8.

Wistow, G. and Barnes, M. (1986) *Ottawa Charter for Health Promotion*. Geneva: World Health Organization.

Wistow, G. and Barnes, M. (1991) 'Community participation for health for all', paper prepared for *UK HFA Network*.

Wistow, G. and Barnes, M. (1993) 'User involvement in community care: origins, purposes and applications', *Public Administration*, 71(3), 279–99.

Wistow, G. and Brooks, T. (eds) (1988) *Joint Planning and Joint Management*. London: Royal Institute for Public Administration.

WHO (1985) *Targets for Health for All*. Copenhagen: World Health Organization Regional Office for Europe.

Woodward, N. (1994) *Public Involvement in Health Care Purchasing. An Investigation of Process*. Southampton: University of Southampton.

# Index

Abelson, J., 121
accountability
  central and local, 38, 42, 55–6, 63,
    71, 72, 87–8, 133
  civil servants, 33–4, 37
  and community health councils,
    69–70, 104, 133
  democratic, 37, 54, 59, 87, 88–9
  eroding checks and balances,
    37–40
  health authorities and, 99
  and healthcare purchasing, 87–9,
    91–2
  modernization of, 33–7
  in the NHS, 40–3, 62, 68, 71
  political, 34–5, 40–3, 98
  and public involvement, 54–6, 107,
    127, 133, 136
*Accountability Framework*, 89, 107,
  130, 131, 132, 133
ACHCEW (Association of Community
  Health Councils for England and
  Wales), 105, 121
Acts of Parliament
  Audit Act (1983), 38
  Education Act (1980), 21
  Education Act (1986), 21
  Education Reform Act (1988), 27–8,
    60
  Health Authorities Act (1995), 81,
    128
  Health and Medicines Act (1988),
    29
  Health Services Act (1980), 21
  Housing Act (1980), 21, 60
  Housing Act (1986), 60
  Housing Act (1988), 28
  Housing and Planning Act (1986),
    21
  Local Government Planning and
    Land Act (1980), 20
  National Health Service
    Reorganisation Act (1973), 68
  NHS and Community Care Act
    (1990), 28, 42, 60–1, 78–9
  NHS Reorganisation Act (1972), 40
  Primary Care Act (1997), 127
Advocacy Alliance, 75–6
advocacy movement, 67, 75–6, 100,
  111, 123, 125
Agass, M., 86, 106
Age Concern, 67–8, 110
Agenda 21, 103, 129
AIMS (Association for Improvements
  in Maternity Services), 67
Alford, R., 90
Alleged Lunatics' Friends Society, 67
Allsop, J., 64